SALES Rx

Daily Prescriptions for Success in Selling

365 Proven Actions
and Timeless Principles
to Guarantee
a Profitable and Fulfilling
Sales Career
**in ANY Industry and in
ALL Market Conditions**

Dale Verseput

outskirts press

SalesRx - Daily Prescriptions for Success in Selling
365 Proven Actions and Timeless Principles to Guarantee a Profitable and Fulfilling Sales Career in ANY Industry and in ALL Market Conditions

v4.0

Outskirts Press, Inc.
http://www.outskirtspress.com

Paperback ISBN: 978-1-9772-6299-8
Hardback ISBN: 978-1-9772-6306-3

PRINTED IN THE UNITED STATES OF AMERICA

To Lisa and Annika,

the greatest gifts of God to me on this earth.

You are a blessing and I love you both.

INTRODUCTION

What happens when the Doctor prescribes the correct medication for your ailment? You take the exact dosage, at the required intervals, for a defined period of time, and voila – you're healed! You feel better, your energy and drive return, and you tell others you're back to your old self. What has occurred internally is that you have built up a therapeutic level of the chemical(s) necessary to destroy the foreign elements which were causing you pain and discomfort. The same can be true for your sales career! I'm certainly no Doctor, but what I prescribe in this book will heal you, energize you, and protect you from future attacks on the health of your sales ability. How do I know this? I've proven over three decades, the efficacy of the elements which make up these prescriptions through not just my own success, but that of countless others who have achieved similar positive results with varying dosages of the same general formula. Remember too, your doctor doesn't typically explain the complex chemical composition of the prescribed medication, or the particular biological pathways it utilizes, or how your body metabolizes it. He asks you to take it because he knows it will work. Such is the same with the prescriptive recommendations within this book. They are not exhaustive explanations inclusive of their supporting philosophies. Rather, they are succinct, tactical directives designed to positively improve your sales acumen and resulting achievements in the shortest duration.

SALES - Is it an Art? Is it a Science? Can selling skills be learned? Are some individuals born with talents and abilities which make them naturally adept at selling? The answer is *YES* to all of the above, which should be great news to everyone. Rewarding careers as Salespeople are available to ALL! Want some even better news? You don't have to be deceitful or manipulative or comfortable with compromising your principles in order to be successful. In fact, it's exactly the opposite. The truth is, in order to maximize your potential success in Sales, you must abandon the heart's penchant for deceit, manipulation, and corrupt behavior, and commit yourself to honesty, integrity, transparency, and truth. To behave otherwise is short-sighted, unsustainable, and ultimately doomed to failure. There are, of course, individuals who practice the nefarious behaviors previously mentioned who have somehow successfully convinced the rest of society that those attributes are universally embraced in the *Selling* trade. That is unfortunate, and also for the consumer, an erroneous assumption.

There are certainly some great thinkers in the world of sales philosophy today. I have chosen to incorporate a select few of their comments which have helped me immensely and which I felt were worthy of repeating, in the pages ahead. There also exists an abundance of so-called *sales experts* in the consultancy space who were successful in certain burgeoning markets of the 80's and 90's. Many of them have since left their fields of expertise and have dedicated their lives to training others how to achieve similar levels of accomplishment. I have found many of them to be either misguided, irrelevant, or just plain wrong in their approach to customers.

I believe they were in the right place at the right time, and this may have given them a false sense that their success was somehow due to their *mad* selling skills. In reality, it's likely they happened to represent products the consuming public was desperate for, and had plans to purchase regardless.

I'm NOT a sales consultant and I don't sell training or seminars. I haven't switched careers or stopped my activities as a commercial leader in my industry to become a keynote speaker or full-time author. The guidance and instruction offered in this book is utilized by myself and my team daily as we continue to develop our skills in this rewarding field. For the first 12 years of my working life, I sold money. It is perhaps the most intangible product to represent... other than cryptocurrency, I guess. I then transitioned to capital equipment sales, but have been tremendously grateful for the financial education I received early in my career. The reason is that so many purchases, irrespective of industry, often get reduced to dollars and cents. Having a command of acquisition methods, from an accounting and financial perspective, can often times mean the difference in whether or not you make the sale.

There are some secrets for sales success I have learned along the way which will always remain safe with me (and my employer). That's just part of the code of a sales professional. However, there are some not-so-secret gems which have helped elevate my personal sales success and which should be in the public domain. In my experience, they will raise the level of competence, professionalism, and ultimate success for those who will embrace them as their own. They are the 365 Proven Actions and Timeless Principles which fill the pages of this book.

Lastly, it's important in sales to remember to be yourself, to embrace technology (the entirety of the first draft of this book was written on my smartphone at an average altitude of 35,000 feet), to read, study, and observe, as you create your own personal brand and selling style. People like to buy from others who are genuine, personable, and similar to themselves. Do I always listen to my doctor and do exactly what he tells me to? No. Admittedly, I don't drink enough water or get as much aerobic exercise as I should. Just like I don't do enough reading. But no matter the endeavor, we can all do better, and my earnest desire is that this book will help you on your journey to becoming a better salesperson.

1

Salespeople are generally well-meaning when they approach customers. But are often poorly trained in how to do so properly, especially when just starting out in their careers. There is perhaps no other statement from a salesperson that engenders a greater sense of naïveté and disingenuity than, *"I can save you money!"* It does not matter what you are selling… stop using that phrase as part of your pitch. You can deliver the same message in a more intelligent manner. The better line would be, *"Our customers often report to us that the greatest benefit they realize from implementing our solution is the significant reduction in total spend."*

2

Character and principles matter. Honesty and integrity will be the strongest building blocks for every future success in your sales career. Commit yourself to being a person known for these attributes. As a consequence, never lie about the product or service you are selling, and never misrepresent its capabilities. If you think you need to…pick a different career.

3

The sales trade is perhaps the most misunderstood, underappreciated, and least recognized of all business disciplines. Many of those outside the sales profession have a distorted view, or no view at all, of what salespeople actually do and what attitudes and actions are required for long-term success. As an example, if you consider playing golf and paying for dinner the primary activities of a successful salesperson…you'll never be one.

4

Most customers have a desire for fresh approaches, new ideas, alternative solutions, and novel strategies. It will take a valiant effort to remain proficient in providing creative options which address the problem(s) your customer is trying to solve. My recommendation is to pray for creativity…and also read books on the subject.

5

The activities of trade and commerce are wide-ranging and far-reaching, with an almost unlimited basket of disciplines available to build competencies in. There are a few core business principles which transcend both professions and industries. One of them is particularly well-suited to the field of sales. It is:

Under-Promise and Over-Deliver…Always!

6

Life doesn't always go as planned…and particularly so in sales it seems. Do not panic when things go bad. React swiftly. Respond sympathetically. Recover thoroughly. Lastly, give your customer something beyond what would reasonably be expected in the course of resolving an unanticipated problem. Successful, properly executed resolutions have the potential to build customer loyalty like almost nothing else.

7

Everyone wants the lowest price, right? Wrong. Everyone wants the *BEST* price. Lowest price and best price are not the same things. It all hinges on what you are actually receiving for what you are paying. As a personal selling principle, resist the temptation to be the low-price supplier. *Price* is the weakest position to sell from, and as a low-price leader, you will typically have little or NOTHING else left to offer.

8

As you might expect, salespeople and their proposals are rebuffed more often than they are accepted. Much more often in most cases. In other words, you will get a *"No"* many more times than you will receive a *"Yes"*. Take heart…there are no new objections in the world of sales, and there haven't been for quite some time. Do a little investigation and find out what the most common ones are in your industry and in the location you serve. When you encounter them, make sure you have deft responses at-the-ready. As you advance in your selling skills, you should strive to craft your approach in such a manner as to prevent the objections from happening in the first place.

9

Salespeople often fall into the trap of *Tunnel Vision*. Too often they focus on a single product offering for a particular customer, when in fact there may be multiple offerings the client could benefit from, or have a need for, in other areas of their business. Another myopic trait is task orientation. Again, often focusing on only one at a time. Selling behaviors and activities should rarely be linear. One example is the installation and commissioning process. While this may seem a straightforward, singular activity, you should never leave a successful new-product delivery without introducing yourself to your customer's neighbors…next door, across the street, floor above, floor below, etc. Always look to every action for the complement of an opportunity to influence a next or future sale. This is part of what is referred to as having a *Sales Mindset*.

10

Your work ethic can and should be a powerful differentiator for you. To the benefit of your customer for sure, but most notably in creating separation vis-à-vis your competitive counterparts. In addition to daytime dominance, work while your competitors are sleeping…or while they're watching late night television. This is often the best time and easiest way to gain ground on them.

11

At a particular time and place, when your potential customer reaches the point where he needs your product or service, you want to be sure you and your solution are top of mind. There's a way to guarantee that you are: Be the most VISIBLE, most WELL-CONNECTED, and most HELPFUL salesperson in your territory of responsibility.

12

Marketing, advertising, and promotion all have a role to fill in overall sales strategy. It's often assumed these activities are the responsibility of a supporting department. When it comes to corporate, product, or industry promotion, many of them are. However, those worthy of your personal attention have to do with building your personal brand and reputation. Here's what I prescribe…Be proactive with your personal and professional promotion. But take care not to let yourself get mired in these activities, and don't waste time being active on any social media platform other than LinkedIn!

13

It is difficult to mask, or completely hide what you're feeling inside. Your body language, verbal cues, and other behaviors usually give you away. This is important to understand if you're going to be a successful salesperson. Here's the lesson: If you don't have a passionate belief in the value of what you are selling, your potential customer will immediately know it. Your attempts at positive persuasion will appear incongruent with how you are unconsciously presenting yourself. Never feign your excitement. Be genuine and *keep it real.*

14

Our mental fitness and the discipline involved in cultivating a healthy thought life has an effect on our physical activity and abilities as well. Many will say, *"Attitude is everything"*. I'm not sure I would agree 100%, but if it's not *everything*, it's certainly of great significance. I think Henry Ford had it right when he posited, *"If you think you can or you think you can't, you're right either way"*.

15

There's often great wisdom to be found in the study of historical figures, their behaviors, and accomplishments. In many ways, the world was a less complicated place centuries ago, and some of what you learn from it can be quite simple, yet profound. The following is an example of exactly that. *"Whatever your hand finds to do, do it with all your might"* - A wise and powerful prescription from King Solomon of Israel (979-931 BC)

16

If you are a Sales Manager, one best practice you should implement is to hold an off-site Sales *Boot Camp* with your team, and benchmark the best answers to the top 3 or 4 customer objections in your territory. Write the answers down, edit them for brevity, optimize them for clarity and linguistic impact, and adopt them as a standard for the sales team. Individual styles and approaches notwithstanding, your team should be unified in how they respond to the most common customer protests.

17

While perhaps somewhat obvious, your value proposition needs to be compelling. The customer should see you as the clear and unchallenged *best* choice. In the course of presenting your solution, tailor your sales conversations with the goal of guiding your customer to a point where you can sincerely ask, *"Why wouldn't you do this?"*

18

Sales is certainly not without nuance, and strategizing on best approaches for individual deals can often be quite cerebral exercises. However, if you want a simple, overarching formula for success…Have the BEST attitude, the BEST product knowledge, and give the BEST service, and you will win more often.

19

Join a Trade Association for one of your target customer's industries. Most of them offer memberships to *Associate* or *Affiliate* companies, which are defined as supporting organizations that supply products or professional services to the particular trade. Be active by getting yourself on a committee and positioning yourself as a resource to other members. In terms of uncovering new opportunities and building relationships with key decision makers, this is some of the lowest hanging fruit across the greatest number of market segments you will ever encounter.

20

Ironically, there are at least elements of both poor planning and impatience, prevalent in almost every industry and organization that exists today. As such, many customers will start asking you for a proposal from your very first meeting with them. It will take some creativity to deny their requests, yet not have them feel slighted. It is best to delay giving a selling price to your potential customer as long as you possibly can. In the interim, spend your time building so much value that when you finally do reveal your price, it will be much less than they expected.

21

Over time, as you mature in your sales career, you will develop skills for determining the proper pace of deal development. At some point, you will begin to know instinctively when to move the customer to the next step, when to slow the process down, or when to ask a particular question, etc. As a starting point, it is unwise to disclose customer references or provide testimonials early in the selling process. Instead, save them until right before you're ready to ask for the order. They should be that part of the *closing* dialogue which adds validity and proof to the claims you have made up to that point.

22

"Your customer will ALWAYS be able to sell your product better than you can." This is a phrase I have uttered countless times over the years to members of my sales teams. The reason I believe this, is because your potential client will view an existing user as instantly credible and will place more validity on their claims than he does yours. There is no need to take offense to this. Instead, leverage this knowledge for your benefit. The takeaway? Harvest customer testimonials regularly…and keep them current.

23

Sales Managers: There are many qualities we can point to as common attributes of successful salespeople. However, your customer(s) will never experience them if they don't first establish a relationship with your representative. Of primary importance is to ensure you can at least get through the door. Therefore, always hire salespeople who are intelligent, happy, and personable. In other words, people who are instantly likable.

24

Never ask your potential customer to tell you about his business...you should already know all about it! Use the incredible online tools available to you through the world wide web. It's the greatest advancement in sales enablement since the advent of the cell phone. Usually, the best pages to study on your potential customer's website are commonly titled:

About Us, History, Who We Are, What We Do, Company Info, and *Our Mission.*

Align your questions, solutions, and stories of success with the principles and goals found on those pages and you will instantly elevate yourself to *preferred* status in your customer's mind.

25

Few things have the ability to alter moods and perceptions better than music. That's because it has been shown to have the power to influence dopamine production in the brain, and also affect heart rate. It has particularly powerful effects when we're listening to music we greatly enjoy. Listen to your favorite Rock Music on the way to your sales presentation. The time for preparation is over. Now is the time to get PUMPED! Get amped up with music that energizes you and walk into your appointment with the confidence of a Rock Star!

26

During the selling process, never be deceptive or manipulative, but be sure you're the one controlling the narrative and guiding the conversations with your prospective client. From initial contact to receiving the purchase order, the most successful salespeople are those who stay in control of leading the sales discussions wire-to-wire.

27

"Demo" Expense can be one of the largest monthly operational cost categories on a Sales Department's financials. If the product you are selling commonly requires demonstration, have your potential customer *Demo* it at YOUR facility instead of hers as often as you can. You will be better able to maintain control of the experience; your customer will get to view your facilities and capabilities up close; key support team members can be personally introduced; and most importantly, both time and capital will be conserved.

28

If there's one thing COVID taught us, it's that there are lots of salespeople who are horrible at making presentations…don't let that be you! Before kicking things off with a "cold open" in front of your customer, take the time to do a run-through with an internal audience who won't be afraid to give you honest, unfettered feedback. Another thing to remember when building your slide deck; with allowance for customer questions and other nuances of live performance, your presentation will most often run 2-3X longer than you originally anticipated. Count on it.

29

Try to avoid using text when composing presentation slide decks. If you do have to use text, for the sake of everyone, don't read it aloud when presenting! The BEST presentations use only High-Resolution, relevant images, as source material for the narrative you want to deliver. These have consistently proven themselves to be the most compelling and impactful. There's a psychological reason why, but just know that it works!

30

There is no shortage of research confirming the opportunity for most of us to improve our listening skills. Indeed, this is often one of the first topics addressed when seeking out professional sales skills training. The best way I've found to show a potential customer you are being attentive to what they are telling you, is by taking notes. Be sure to use a tablet with an electronic pencil and NOT a paper note pad. Your customer needs to know not only that you are listening, but that you are also technologically current.

31

Optimism is an admirable trait and I encourage cultivating a healthy attitude of such. However, never let your optimism cloud your prudent judgment or disconnect you from reality. As an example, do not convince yourself a verbal approval from your customer is anything other than an indication you are possibly still being considered. You don't have a sale until you have a signed proposal, a purchase order, or a deposit…and sometimes all three!

32

Authenticity reigns supreme when initiating sales conversations with your potential customer. Abandon the use of your employer's recommended greetings, salutations, or conversation starters, which are most often corny and disingenuous…unless you can deliver them with heartfelt sincerity, and they fit with your personality and normal pattern of speaking.

33

Here is a universal truth worth remembering - If you sell a mechanized product which requires periodic maintenance, *Sales* sells the first one…*Parts, Service, or Customer Support* sell the rest. In other words, you could have done yeoman's work in pitching your product and convincing the customer of its superior value. But if you're not providing stellar support after it gets delivered, you can forget about any future orders. In fact, your company should think of itself first as a *service* organization, and secondarily as a *sales* entity. It's the quality and level of customer support which is most often the greatest determinant of whether or not a repeat purchase ever takes place.

34

Are you new to Sales? Here's some sound advice once shared with me early in my career…Focus on taking care of your customer, and your commissions will take care of themselves. Allow yourself to fall into the trap of calculating your potential compensation with every opportunity that comes your way, and you won't get more than two hours of sleep at night.

35

Make the most of any downtime you might have during the workday. Read books on Selling, Marketing, Customer Loyalty, Creativity, Service & Support, Organization, and Time Management. There are thousands of them out there, and you're probably not reading enough of them. They have the power to transform both your mindset and your career.

36

Is your Service Manager giving you a hard time about wanting to give things away? Too often, Sales and Service departments are completely disconnected from each other, working at cross purposes, and failing to understand what it is each other needs in order to preserve customer relationships. Here's a thought - next time take him with you to visit the customer together and see how tough he is when you're all in the same room.

37

Let your pricing be fair and firm from the very beginning, and respectfully remind your customer she should be demanding the same of every potential supplier being considered. As a corollary, if you have the authority to make concessions and/or adjust pricing on the spot, but your customer contact lacks the power to accept the same…then your negotiation is not an equitable one. This is an all too common and unfortunate symptom of not dealing directly with decision makers.

38

The psychology of selling and the human interaction involved in the process is a distinct and important discipline to be sure. However, it is not of a particular focus in this book. Suffice to say, enough long-term studies have now been concluded which clearly show the most successful salespeople are those with a high competency in Emotional and Social Intelligence (ESI).

39

A gift, a surprise, a bonus! Almost everyone enjoys receiving a little something *extra*. When you finally make delivery of your product, give the customer something additional of value they were not expecting. It's the best way to kick off a new relationship and to make the process memorable for them…and that should always be one of your goals.

40

The Apostle Paul displayed arguably the greatest work ethic of all time when he pronounced, "*Whatever you do, work at it with all your heart, as though you were working for the Lord and not for people*" Whether you are an adherent of Christianity or not, the point is well made that you should have a greater purpose for doing what you do, beyond simply pleasing your employer or collecting a paycheck.

41

Mentioned elsewhere in this book is the power that proper sleep, listening to music, physical exercise, and other immaterial activities can have on our psyche. Here is a very tangible and material prescription which can yield similar dramatic effect: Wear clothes that make you feel confident in your appearance and proud of how you present yourself…especially on Presentation Day. Knowing you look *sharp* can be empowering on many levels.

42

Be Funny…Be Genuine…Be Yourself

The customer knows when you're *posing*.

43

Sales can, in a very real sense, be accurately described as a competition, a battle, or a race. Separation from those you are competing against is necessary to gain the opportunity for a *win*. That separation is achieved by being different. Differentiation is often considered the Holy Grail of sales success. Make sure you have some and can clearly articulate what it is. *(More on this later)*

44

If you look like you know where you are going or what you are supposed to be doing, human nature tends to compel others not to question. Harness this fact to the benefit of your selling ability. Walk with confidence and purpose and with an accompanying demeanor, and you will gain access your competitors only dream about…or sheepishly ask permission for.

45

Never expect sales orders to just come to you. Yes, with longevity in your field, great customer relationships, and a reputation for fairness and value, there will be a point at which opportunities seem to just start presenting themselves. That is the ultimate goal of your continued and consistent selling efforts. But don't let yourself be fooled by the occasional serendipitous deal. Success will not be found without energy, effort, and proactivity. You will have to go get the business. Fortune favors the bold! Sales is not a career for the shy or introverted.

46

In sales, the importance of adequate preparation cannot be overstated. Preparing for presentations; learning the best answers to common objections; Setting periodic goals, plans, and objectives; Strategizing how to best approach a particular prospect. These are all important steps in preparing yourself for success in selling. The following statement sums it up perhaps the most succinctly.

"Well begun is half done"

\- Mary Poppins

47

Don't waste time searching for a silver bullet, crystal ball, or magical solution. There is no single BEST sales strategy, method, or tactic. There are TONS of them, and they can all work well from time to time. Study as many of them as you can and then personalize them, practice them, and employ elements of them when and where appropriate.

48

The RFQ was issued almost 60 days ago and you're just finding out about it now? It's becoming all too common for suppliers to gain first awareness of bid solicitations in the eleventh hour. What then ensues is a mad scramble to pull everything and everyone together to rush forward a proposal which meets the required specifications. That is not an environment conducive to doing your best work. It's an unfortunate outcome of most salespeople's tendency to be reactionary. Reactivity is not a growth-oriented behavior. Do whatever is necessary for you to stay ahead of the game and to be proactive in your efforts to sell. When that RFQ does get issued, it should be built around YOUR specifications, not your competitor.

49

There are significant differences between selling industry-standard, mid-grade products, and those considered best-in-class or *premium*. Most salespeople lack the necessary skills to maintain consistent success at selling premium. If through your command of Emotional Intelligence you have a self-awareness of this, seek out training on how to have the highest price…and WIN! Those are the skills which separate the professional salesperson from the apprentice.

50

Being brief and concise always helps drive home a point or put emphasis on a statement. Consequently, it also makes what you are presenting more memorable to your customer. Here is an axiom for sales presentations, written or verbal…The more time you have to prepare, the fewer words should be used.

51

Stay coachable! There should never come a day when you feel you've learned all there is to know about sales and selling, or that you simply know enough. You may indeed have achieved mastery of your craft, but even the most skilled professional wisely keeps himself on a path of continuous improvement. Think about it…no matter the sport, most professional athletes can outscore and outperform their coaches in a head-to-head matchup on any given day. That's because submission to another with a superior skillset is not the obligatory criteria for retaining a coach. Instead, it is for the purpose of being able to accomplish more than you could on your own.

52

Arrogance will cost you more business than almost anything else. Approach your craft and your customers confidently, yet with humility.

53

Customer Care, Aftermarket Support, Service & Repair. These are all departments which can behave in relatively the same manner year after year, yet still produce satisfactory results. The Sales Department, on the other hand, is typically the most intellectually rigorous department in the company. Why? Because we have to continually reinvent ourselves in order to remain relevant…and it's more difficult than you might think. Make sure you're up for the challenge.

54

It's been said that no matter what job you have in life, your success will be determined 5% by your academic credentials, 15% by your professional experiences, and 80% by your communication skills. Study language and syntax, and aspire to become a bit of a *wordsmith*. Words have meaning, and this may prove no truer than in the realm of sales and selling. This is a surefire way to create competitive separation. Your customer will judge you by how well you speak and write… and so will your bank account.

55

Attention Sales Managers! - The high-performing, over-achieving sales personality profile is typically task-averse to paperwork, reporting, call-logging, budgeting, and bureaucratic minutiae. If you're insistent on requiring they do all of the above anyway, then prepare to lose a star performer...or simply pay for her to have a dedicated admin.

56

If through the commission program your company occasionally has salespeople with higher incomes than their department managers, that's generally a sign of a healthy organization that is focused on growing their business. Individuals harboring *Old School* management logic will be vehemently opposed to such, however. Just be aware.

57

Not much time will be spent on these pages getting *into the weeds* of how to best respond to common sales objections. In spite of that, here's a brief and effective retort for your price-obsessed customer: *"When has going with the lowest price ever been a GREAT business decision?"*

58

You will always have three critical areas of differentiation available to you:

Yourself - Your Company or Brand - Your Product or Service. If you are lacking in any one of these three areas, don't despair...It just means you will need to work harder on creating greater separation in the other two.

59

Too often, salespeople are fickle. Sometimes it's the result of their employer not recognizing the importance of, and properly supporting the Sales Department or the Field Sales Team specifically. Nevertheless, customers have become accustomed to short-term relationships with salespeople and tend to view them as opportunists who are always chasing a dollar. This is unfortunate and needs to be changed. Here's the charge…First and foremost, focus on building Long-Term relationships with your clients…Always!

60

Be a resource first and a salesperson second. Establishing yourself as a "go-to" source of information and advice, without expecting anything in return, will cause your social capital to skyrocket...and that's relationship Gold!

61

Stock investments, marriage, raising kids, working towards a big promotion…these are all endeavors where the common advice is to *play the long game*. Well, I would add that in Sales and Selling there are also no shortcuts. The most successful salespeople in any industry tend to be those with the greatest longevity. It makes sense. (see Rx #59)

62

NEVER turn down an invitation to speak to an audience. In fact, seek out and volunteer yourself for those opportunities whenever possible. Resourcefulness, visibility, presentation skills, credibility, wit, and improvisation can all be enhanced and honed through the medium of public speaking.

63

You will no doubt get caught up in a whirlwind of activity soon enough when entering a career in sales. Never let yourself get too deep into the forest as to no longer be able to see the trees, as they say. It's important to maintain perspective. Let the following principle guide you...work only *FOR* your customer, and only *WITH* a company or individual that genuinely appreciates you.

64

I'm not completely convinced we are only six or fewer acquaintance links apart, as the informal law popularized by Kevin Bacon would have us believe. Nevertheless, we do live in a world of interconnectivity. Make sure both you and your Marketing Department are taking maximum advantage of the LinkedIn business networking platform. A subscription to their *Sales Navigator* feature is an absolute must.

65

Most of us desire the quickest path to improvement, no matter the endeavor in life. Regular physical exercise can do more than almost any other activity in keeping both your mind and your selling skills sharp! My cardiologist tells me 150 minutes per week is ideal.

66

What's the best way to demonstrate your product or service? Consider the words of the late German composer Carl Orff, *"Tell me, and I forget. Show me, and I remember. Involve me, and I understand."* The more interactive you can make the demonstration, physically involving your customer in some sort of process or activity, the more lasting impact it will have.

67

Some customers erroneously place greater importance on a product's warranty statement than they do the manufacturer's credibility or the production quality of the underlying item. Take effort not to allow your client to linger in this area during the sales process. Your competitors can play numerous games with warranty terms through accounting methods and other financial offsets or reserves. Besides, if you have done an adequate job presenting and assuring the quality of your product throughout each stage of the customer's buying cycle, warranty terms should not be high on their list of concerns. To paraphrase the late Chris Farley's dynamo sales character, Tommy Callahan, *"I can take a crap in a box and put a warranty on it for ya…but then all you've got is a guaranteed piece of sh*t."*

68

ALWAYS find out why you won a deal or why you lost a deal. If you're on the losing side, it will no doubt prove more difficult to get the information from the previously sought customer. But you should try anyway. As you build a history of this transaction intelligence, do more of what you find causes you to win and less of that which tends to make you lose…I call it Sales Optimization.

69

My personal Sales, Marketing, and Management heroes are Jeffrey Gitomer, Joe Calloway, Mike Abrashoff, Jason Jordan, Ellen Rohr, Robert O. Heavner, John Uprichard, Wym Portman, Kerry Bodine, Bob Tasca, John Ruskin, John Patterson, and Larry Steinmetz. Many of them have written extensively on their areas of expertise. Purchase their books and avail yourself of their wisdom as you work on developing your own sales ideology.

70

Be certain you are not asking the same questions of prospective clients your competitors are. Work on coming up with relevant and meaningful questions your potential customer has likely never heard before. This is a fantastic practice for creating separation between yourself and your competitive counterparts, whom customers tend to view as all the same.

71

The advent of lightning-fast, global communication, through the vehicle of worldwide electronic connectivity, is both a blessing and a curse. The *curse* portion being it has increased the frequency of passionate, emotion-filled reaction, when a delayed, measured, and more thoughtful response would have been the wiser path. In short, resist the urge to share political, religious, or environmental viewpoints via email or social media!

72

Being in sales is never career-limiting or without opportunity for advancement. It is in fact, quite the contrary. Beyond being a springboard for professional growth, which it most often is, developing strong selling skills can help you in almost ANY role and in ANY industry you might find yourself in throughout your working years.

73

In my experience, many salespeople shy away from acknowledging the need to run their businesses similar to their customers. It's an important perspective to understand that you both want to provide a great product or service, to have happy employees, to give value to your customers and to the communities you serve…and to be PROFITABLE! Your customers expect that. It is absolutely necessary as a strong and capable supplier, to be evolving, growing, advancing, and profiting. Have the courage to make a profit!

74

There are a million different ways to *ask for the order* from your customer. Some of them are sad and pathetic. Others can be quite creative and brilliant. Nevertheless, the fact of the asking remains a necessary requirement for success in selling. Don't ever shy away from it. When asking for the order, an often-successful prefacing comment I have used numerous times is, *"With your permission, I would like to..."*

75

Commit the entirety of the following quotation to memory and refresh it often in your mind. You will begin to find yourself repeatedly referring to at least portions of it during the course of almost all future customer conversations.

"There is hardly anything in the world that someone cannot make a little worse and sell a little cheaper, and the people who consider price alone are that person's lawful prey. It's unwise to pay too much, but it's worse to pay too little. When you pay too much, you lose a little money – that is all. When you pay too little, you sometimes lose everything, because the thing you bought was incapable of doing the thing it was bought to do. The common law of business balance prohibits paying a little and getting a lot – it cannot be done. If you deal with the lowest bidder, it is wise to add something for the risk you run, and if you do that, you will have enough to pay for something better."

– John Ruskin

76

Were you or your team not able to perform as was promised when you were awarded the sale? It's always best to address the non-performance or poor performance issues in person. Never offer remedies or excuses over the phone or via email. If the customer needs to get their *pound of flesh* out of you…let them.

77

Your customer doesn't care how busy you are, how short-handed you may be, how your suppliers didn't perform, or if the rest of your industry suffers from the same ills. If you failed to meet the expectations that were set, you have an obligation to *make it right* for your customer. There is no valid argument supporting otherwise.

78

The old adage is true (probably why it's considered an old adage) – Take good care of your customers…or someone else will.

79

Purchasing and Procurement Managers are trained and educated to maintain control of only one thing…PRICE. As much as they may protest the validity of that accusation, never let them convince you otherwise.

80

My Key Account Manager and I once visited a customer AFTER a purchase order had already been issued to our competitor for a much cheaper piece of equipment. We were more than just late to the party. The party was already over. On top of that, the wife of the competitor's salesperson worked in the customer's accounting department. It was going to be an uphill battle for sure. Instead of meeting with the purchasing manager, we met with Gerry, the VP & Plant Manager. In brief, our day ended with the competitor's sale being cancelled, and we left with a new purchase order of our own for close to double the amount! The Purchasing Manager's reply? *"If Gerry is OK with it, then so am I"*. There are several key selling principles which were confirmed by our meeting that day. But this is probably the biggest takeaway...If you're dealing directly with the person responsible for the P&L, then even a Certified Purchasing Manager (CPM) can be told who to buy from.

81

Start your selling efforts as early in the buying cycle and at as high a level in the customer organization as you possibly can. That's the sweet spot for maximizing your influence over the ultimate purchasing decision, and the best opportunity to build value and justification for your premium solution.

82

If a potential customer calls in the eleventh hour seeking one last bid to close out his RFQ, you have only two options; 1. Don't oblige, or 2. Send over the quote with a healthy margin, then save it to a virtual file folder and forget about it. Don't follow up, don't call or email, and don't put it in your forecast. If you end up winning the deal, consider it good fortune.

83

First or last…which is best? All things being equal, I almost always prefer to be the first to make a pitch. You should know who you will be competing against, and you should also know exactly how they will present themselves and their solution. Going first allows you to completely steal their thunder by prepping the customer on what they should expect to hear, and also to set their expectations high through a brilliant presentation. *First impressions are lasting impressions* is a time-honored maxim for good reason.

84

It is most often a non-decision maker who is tasked with collecting proposals from prospective suppliers. With respect to your product or service, no one can *Tell it or Sell it* like you can. NEVER let some quote harvester at the potential customer attempt to make the pitch to the decision maker on your behalf. That is an exercise only YOU can properly and professionally execute.

85

Is your customer asking for a credit? Try starting the conversation with, *"What do you think is fair?"* You'll be surprised how often they answer with an amount lower than you expected.

86

While it is exponentially easier to establish first contact with junior management members at your potential customer, it will at the same time increase the level of difficulty in getting your value proposition to the individuals who actually need to hear it. The wiser path is to increase your chances of success by first putting yourself in front of decision makers and check writers. In other words, people with the power to say, *"Let's do it!"*

87

Rich M. was a supervisor of mine early in my career. Rich had a son who was a decorated Sheriff's Deputy, regularly lauded for his unprecedented seizure rate in the recovery of illegal firearms and narcotics. When questioned about the secret to his success, Rich's son replied, *"There is no secret…I just ask 'em"*. Whether a routine traffic stop or a number of other seemingly innocuous interactions, he would never conclude his interviews without asking if the suspect had any drugs or firearms on their person or in their vehicle. Whether out of compulsion never to lie to a law enforcement officer, or assuming a search was likely inevitable, the frequency of the answer being *"Yes"* was staggering. Even those charged with protecting us can benefit from the most basic, yet critical selling prescription…Ask for the order - ALWAYS ask for the order!

88

Be as helpful as you can be during the very first contact with your potential customer. It could be in the form of educating them on what to expect during the process they are launching into, or perhaps you could offer to introduce them to one of your existing clients whom they've been trying to establish a relationship with themselves. It could even be helping them determine you're not the best partner for their current project. Whatever it is, strive to provide value to your potential customer before anything else. What is something of value? Anything that is of marginal cost to you, but of high(er) worth to your client.

89

Do your competitors hate your guts and wish you were dead? Congratulations! Don't feel bad. Instead, be encouraged by the wisdom of Ambrose Bierce, *"Contempt is the emotion one feels for an opponent whose arguments are too formidable to refute."*

90

Competitive advantages are great…but they NEVER last. If you've got some, exploit them while you can!

91

There is a time and place for Feature & Benefit discussions as well as education. You certainly need to know what yours are, and they should at least be a component of your overall value proposition. However, too often this has become the entirety of product sales training. Particularly in the Manufacturer-Distributor business model. The factory sales trainer spends all his time on what he thinks are the big differentiators for success, and little or no time on objection prevention, opportunity qualification, purchase justification, conversation control, or how to ask for the order. Remember, every one of your competitors has Features & Benefits. Your customer may or may not see yours as better than the alternative. If you're going to rely on yours as the bulk of your pitch, be prepared for a low conversion rate. Here's a freebie:

"...Speed is always a cool product feature"

– Ellen Rohr

92

In the Fall of 2015, I took on a new leadership role for a regional team of capital equipment sales representatives. One of those reps was eager to show me the sales quotation template they had recently developed, as it was quite detailed and apparently a marked improvement over the previous version. Prominently displayed on the front page was a large, representative photo of the equipment make and model being proposed. However, it was not a high-resolution image, and in the bottom right-hand corner was the Copyright watermark, "© 2005". So, what's my first question as a potential customer? *"You haven't made any changes or improvements to your product in 10 years?!"*. This was a glaring example of the mediocrity which is so pervasive among sales teams. To borrow some wisdom from the King of Sales, Jeffrey Gitomer, conduct a "quality" audit and eliminate anything in your sales life that isn't *BEST.* If you don't have the best products, the best-looking proposals, the best people on the team, the best processes, or the best training, then replace them with what is... and sooner rather than later is always - BEST!

93

In Sales, every day and sometimes every hour, is precious. From signed order to final delivery, a million things can happen which could cause delay, disruption, or even cancellation of your sale. Things which are sometimes impossible to anticipate or mitigate. No matter how cliché this may sound, always treat the entire process with a sense of urgency and NEVER put off until tomorrow what you can get done today!

94

Are you a Sales*man*? Never wear a button-down short-sleeve dress shirt. That's a man on his way down.

95

In sales you are often required to make judgment calls *on the fly*. It's easier said than done, particularly when you are just starting out. But be encouraged not to waste time or energy second-guessing yourself. Allowing yourself to be plagued with indecision can do great harm to your sales momentum. Make informed decisions with the best data you have available to you at the time, and let the results be what they are.

96

Attention Sales Managers! - There's nothing more embarrassing than having to run to mommy or daddy for an answer. It also destroys the credibility of your salesperson when in front of the customer. Don't force your salespeople to always ask permission. Give them the autonomy and authority to make decisions on the spot. Here's the criteria: Does it benefit the customer? Does it generate a profit? If the answer is *Yes* to both, then ALWAYS back their decision.

97

Everyone in your organization should be empowered with the authority to do what's necessary to make the customer satisfied and happy, even if it means writing a check or issuing a credit. However, they all need to know that with authority comes responsibility. They need to be able to clearly explain the justification for their decision. Too often, protracted handwringing while trying to determine whether or not the customer has a legitimate complaint, or which department is going to be charged, results in the same resolution which could have been made extemporaneously without subjecting the customer to your internal dysfunction.

98

A bit of career advice - Don't just take the first sales job that comes along. It's worth holding out for something you can get passionate about. When you are genuinely excited about the products and solutions you offer to the market, you will be amazed at how compelling you can be when presenting them to your potential customers.

99

Control over establishing competitive separation is greatest when it pertains to yourself. When seeking to achieve personal differentiation, the best way to set yourself apart from your competitive counterparts is through the questions you ask. Yours should be intelligent, relevant, compelling, and unique.

100

Prepare to experience the challenges of creating personal connection from the very first attempt at customer contact. Whether it be phone, email, or in-person, most companies have put barriers in place to prevent the intrusion of the unsolicited sales call. This is why connection through referral or recommendation is so vital. However, as with most sales challenges, getting through the gate is not insurmountable. It once again requires creativity and forethought. Don't be afraid of the gatekeeper…just be smarter!

101

How many times have you said, *"I could have thought of that"*? Then why didn't you? My theory is that we have been conditioned to believe real work only happens when in combination with physical activity. In reality, the ones who can come up with the best strategies and ideas, and then successfully implement them, are usually the market leaders. Set aside time in your daily or weekly schedule to simply THINK and to contemplate. Not about where to go for dinner or summer vacation, but about your market, your product offering, your competitors, industry trends, etc. and what you might do differently to create value and separation.

102

Salespeople sometimes like to keep their selling activities close to the vest. Historically, it's been out of a desire to maintain singular control of the process, or to prevent public knowledge of the customer's pending purchase. In reality, you can't do it all on your own, and the customer isn't secretly trying to work only with you. A mentor once cautioned me, *"Never lose a big deal on your own."* What she meant was…arrogance and secrecy can cause the otherwise skillful salesperson to forfeit a great deal of business. Don't be afraid to engage additional stakeholders in pursuit of the big *WIN*.

103

Take a class, read a book, or watch a video on social intelligence. There's nothing more off-putting to a potential customer than you being completely unaware they ended your meeting 15 minutes ago.

104

Listen more. Talk less. When it IS time to speak, pause 2 or 3 seconds before beginning.

105

Are you a Sales*woman*? Your gender WILL open more doors for you. That's just a reality of today's world. But be sure that's not the only card you have to play…use your brains, not your boobs.

106

Listen and learn from professional sales trainers, but with a healthy level of ponderment and thoughts of how to individualize their recommendations. What you learn from them will help you shape your personal sales philosophy, but it needs to be yours, not theirs.

107

Experience is the best teacher. Think back on buying encounters of your own, and specifically, those things which turned you off or made you go somewhere else. Make sure you're not unknowingly doing the same to YOUR potential customers.

108

People love to give advice. If you've ever played golf in a foursome or tried to get up on waterskis, you know exactly what I'm talking about. The selling trade is no different. You will inevitably hear a couple of cautionary phrases repeated to you often in your sales career, *"Buyers are Liars"* and *"Salespeople are only motivated by money"*. Ignore these statements and the people who make them.

109

Make challenging, but reachable sales goals for yourself. It's motivating to have something to shoot for. You'll be assigned one or more targets by your employer anyway, but they're often not as challenging or as impactful as the ones you set personally.

110

Making a conscious decision and commitment to put in the hard work necessary to ensure success is what will separate you from the other 99% who simply talk a good game. Thomas Edison was on the money when he said, *"If we all achieved what we were capable of, we would literally astound ourselves."* The implication is that most of us are not willing to do what's required to maximize our own potential…but that's only the other guys, right?

111

Paradoxical as it may seem, diversity is the source of harmony in human relationships. In other words, we don't all want the same things at the same time...and that's a good thing! Don't assume your customers are any different. Spend time learning what their likes, dislikes, hot buttons, wants, needs, and goals are, and then...position yourself and your product or service accordingly.

112

It is better to be referred by a member of the C-Suite to a director or manager, than to start your selling process with a lower-level contact and plead for an audience with a decision maker…a sales proverb worth remembering.

113

If your potential customer asks you to give him your best price, do exactly that. If he subsequently asks you to *"sharpen your pencil"* or to *"see what more you can do"*, STAND YOUR GROUND! Don't fall into that trap, don't perpetuate that ridiculous norm of behavior, and respectfully remind him of your adherence to his original request.

114

New to Sales? New to your product? New to your employer? Lack of experience, product knowledge, or process expertise can usually be overcome with enthusiasm, quick wit, and optimism. Maintain all three as a sales veteran and you'll be the big dog everyone is gunning for.

115

The more successful you are, the bigger the target you become. As your market share increases, so does the competition's desire to remove it from you. Positive commercial growth trends become increasingly difficult to maintain the longer they are achieved… Beware and Be Ready.

116

The power of simplicity and consistency is often underappreciated. Sometimes it's better to offer just ONE product or service and be the absolute BEST at it. Example: In-N-Out Burger!

117

Are you selling a premium product that gets delivered in a box? Don't skimp on the packaging. The *Cool* factor of your widget should be reflected in its initial presentation. Buy ANYTHING from Apple and you'll understand.

118

One of the attractive aspects of being in sales is that you can often get by just fine by only working half-days…and you get to pick whichever 12-hour period you want.

119

The importance of a balanced life (Mental – Physical – Spiritual – Relational) as a contributor to career success, is probably no more relevant than in the occupation of sales and selling. A deficiency in even one area can negatively affect your ability to function at peak performance.

120

Use humor to put yourself and your customer at ease during the sales call or sales presentation activity. That doesn't mean telling a few jokes well. It means learning to appropriately employ wit, satire, juxtaposition, anecdote, or self-deprecation... Some have to work on competence in this area more than others.

121

Get ready for the objections, the refusals, the non-commitments, the cancellations, the early terminations, the no-shows, the stalls, the false pretenses, the delays, and the losses, because they are most certainly coming. Condition yourself to treat every *"No"* as a *"Not Yet"* and you'll have the best chance of survival. Getting excited?

122

"Nothing happens until someone sells something"

– Henry Ford

123

Don't consider family and friends two of your target markets. Instead, keep them at arm's length when it comes to business. It's rude to impose a sense of obligation on them, and you shouldn't want the pretense of your personal relationships to be financial gain. You can now safely infer my opinion of multi-level marketing.

124

Does your company sell a product or service and employ salespeople to do so? If yes, you should make processing an order the simplest, least time-consuming, and most enjoyable task in your organization. Don't force your salespeople to sell harder internally than they do with your customers.

125

Manufacturers: Don't let your Engineering department become the Sales Prevention department. Is your sales team screaming that it takes too long to get engineering requests processed? Listen to them! Speed to market, or a lack thereof, can often determine your survivability.

126

The late pioneering Ford dealer, Bob Tasca, liked to describe ordering inventory as basically placing a bet on your future. He was correct in that you will not have the success you hope to have without being able to deliver product in a timely manner. This is true for manufacturers, wholesalers, and retailers alike. Speed to market is critical in so many highly competitive industries, and having a healthy *Stock* inventory of product is a great motivator for sales.

127

If it is to come true, it's up to you! Take personal responsibility for your sales actions. Don't blame lack of training, inadequate support, no inventory, the competition, or the economy. These factors may all be legitimate business concerns, but they can also ALL be conquered with energy and creativity...something lesser salespeople are unable to sustain.

128

Take care of those who take care of you. The value of strong social capital among your support team members is incalculable.

129

Dedicate yourself to being a lifelong learner. Study the market, study the competition, study people and their behavior, and study your trade. Learn something new every day. Practice it, personalize it, employ it, and you won't need too many days before positive results begin to magically appear.

130

There's an axiom in business that says Low Price = Low Profit. You might do well to remind your potential customer that lower-priced competitors will likely not have the resources or the capabilities to support them in the way they will demand. Lack of capital doesn't allow for that.

131

Avoid printed product brochures, spec sheets, proposals, and presentation folders. AFTER you make your pitch, distribute the above to your potential customer in PDF format on company-branded flash drives. It's no longer the 80's.

132

Abandon the idea of making a sale while on a cold call. If you're going to be rude and make an unscheduled visit, it should simply be to gather names and information to assist you in scheduling a future appointment.

133

There are three individuals who do not enjoy unscheduled interruptions during their workday…you, me, and your potential customer. If it's important to discuss, it's worth making an appointment for. It's OK to arrange it by phone, but be sure to formalize it by sending a *meeting invite* via your email client.

134

Authenticity, Sincerity, Relatability, and True Stories will always trump whatever selling *system* or methodology you may think you need to employ.

135

If someone tells you, *"Sales is a numbers game"*, what they mean is - the more customer contacts you make…the more opportunities you will uncover - the more opportunities…the more potential proposals - the more proposals…the more potential *Wins.* In other words, keep filling the funnel. But remember, sales is not ONLY a numbers game. As is prescribed elsewhere, unless relationship and rapport is first established, the opportunities, proposals, and potential wins will never be realized.

136

Never make excuses for your selling price. Remember this: If you're just a little bit higher than your competitor, you will generally be viewed as simply too expensive. If you are significantly higher, it will often invoke a higher perceived value in the mind of your potential customer. It then becomes your responsibility to speak to it and justify it.

137

Buyers, Purchasing Managers, and Procurement Professionals need answers. They are being peppered with questions from their internal stakeholders, wanting to make sure they buy them the right stuff. Make sure you've got the answers! Technical answers, application answers, feature and benefit answers, acquisition answers, delivery answers...you get the point. Here's a tip - Learn what the most common questions generally are and answer them before they are asked. It's called making it easy to do business with you.

138

Whether you refer to it as intellectual honesty, being true to yourself, or simply authenticity, it's important these principles be evident when presenting your solution. Don't sell, represent, promote, or advocate for any product or service, unless you believe in your heart it's the BEST.

139

Chances are, when you're leading a customer through their buying cycle, it will tend to dominate your thoughts. Your brain doesn't turn off when you go to bed at night. More often that's when it does its best work. You would be wise to keep your smartphone or tablet on your nightstand to immediately record the answers, ideas, and strategies you will inevitably wake up with.

140

As much as you might think the answer would give you some straightforward direction, NEVER ask a customer, *"What's it going to take to get your business?"* I could give you three guesses as to how she would respond, and you wouldn't need the first two.

141

There are numerous so-called *Sales Experts* (for many, this moniker is self-ascribed) who would say you need to have an "elevator pitch". Okay…I'll jump on that wagon too. It's good to have one. However, don't even think about starting with, *"I sell* ____________." You're better than that.

142

PRICE - It's the #1 objection in sales and probably always will be. However, it's not often legitimate or valid. But it is the low hanging fruit the buyer's mind will run to and grab hold of if given the opportunity. Your job is to deny him the opportunity.

143

Salespeople often get accused of wanting to give stuff away. Indeed, some individuals outside the selling profession wrongly think it is a common component of sales strategy. The professional salesperson understands there are occasionally times when concession can be wisely used to achieve greater end results. Joe Calloway probably said it best when discussing the power of creating loyal customers, *"...And it doesn't mean giving away the store. But once in a while, give away a piece of the store..."*

144

If you travel even somewhat regularly via airplane for your sales role, purchase an airline club membership from the carrier(s) you patronize most often. Whether your employer compensates you for this or not, is irrelevant. The benefits of club membership for the sales professional are too numerous to list. Email me if you need justification to pull the trigger.

145

Salespeople: Take a deep breath before you immediately spurn the modern CRM software platform. If you have any history of success in sales, then you are already managing customer relationships in some manner. Your employer is simply asking you to migrate those activities into a 21st century medium.

146

Sales Leadership - PLEASE read Jason Jordan's *Cracking The Sales Management Code* before you develop policies around how your organization intends to utilize software CRM. If it's too late for that, read Jason's book anyway and reevaluate your current practices.

147

Never allow your time to be wasted by anyone. It is the one most precious and valuable resource in life which can never be recovered. If you are being forced to wait 15 minutes or longer, you should reschedule or cancel the given activity altogether.

148

As a sales professional, you will need to get educated on financial merchandising as well as accounting methods pertaining to asset acquisition. It is necessary to understand and be able to speak the language of finance, accounting, and taxation. IRR, NPV, ROI, Capitalization, Depreciation, Off-Balance Sheet, and Expensing are all terms you should be comfortable explaining.

149

More and more, customer decisions on whether or not to acquire your product or service are being determined by the results of a financial exercise. Notice I said *acquire* and not *purchase*. There are multiple ways for customers to utilize your offering without buying it. Be sure you know what they are.

150

Are you selling capital equipment? If so, one of the first questions you should ask your prospective client is whether or not they want ownership of the product(s) being considered. If the answer is *"No"*, then there is no valid reason for them to know the cash purchase price of the items, and there is no reason you should want to provide it. At this point, the only thing under consideration, and the only pricing that should be discussed, is monthly, quarterly, or annual payment.

151

Pay attention to stay in your lane. It's OK to test boundaries and push the limits of company policy in the pursuit of caring for your customer. But make an effort to not be viewed as the renegade sales rep. In time, when backed up by solid performance, you'll be given latitude to manage your business in your own way. As my friend Jim Taft once gently reminded me, *"Good policies allow for the occasional exception"*. This is an important point to remember in your journey toward building a strong sales acumen.

152

Don't present proposals which enumerate every acquisition method you offer and think you're doing your customer a favor by being thorough. What you ARE doing is being lazy, not thinking critically, creating confusion, prompting unnecessary questions, and taking leverage and power away from yourself. This is the practice of a weak and improperly trained salesperson…and it happens all the time.

153

Here's a foundational and thought-provoking question which is healthy to ask yourself whenever approaching a new customer, a new opportunity, or both: *"Of the numerous alternatives available to them, why should they buy from me?"* If your customer is savvy, he will likely think to ask you that question at some point. Often in the beginning. You must be able to formulate and articulate cogent arguments which will compel him to prefer you over the others. Periodically spend time contemplating your answer to that question as you cultivate and grow your unique value proposition.

154

Even if you are not exhibiting, it's a good idea to attend industry trade shows for other reasons. Some of them are…to get names and key contacts of potential customers, to examine the competition up-close, to keep yourself current on industry trends, to renew relationships and share stories of success with friends and colleagues in the business, and to keep yourself visible and connected.

155

It's human nature to choose the path of least resistance. We are also *wired* in such a way as to take comfort in the uniformity and consistency of the routine. Your awareness of, and resistance to these patterns will be a key factor in your growth and success. The sales industry is rife with people who do the same things over and over again. Work towards, and take pride in being a differentiator, a change agent, an ideator, a thought leader, and an unorthodox thinker.

156

Pain points, hot buttons, burning platforms, etc. Every customer has them in varying amounts and to varying degrees. Find out what they are, then position yourself and present your product or service in a way that offers remedies. The sooner you can do this, the faster you will separate yourself from those competing for the same opportunity. Experience and practice are the only ways this skillset gets honed. Be patient.

157

Here's a question for the sales leadership team: Are you *Sales Managers*, or have you become *Deal Managers*? The former helps create the conditions which inspire customers to want to buy from you; ensures the internal processing of an order is the least time-intensive component of the selling process; leads his team by example through co-selling, coaching, presenting, and closing. The latter, in contrast, tends to spend lots of time in the office, is the arbiter of discounting and price concessions, and spends the majority of his time gathering data from the field sales team in order to prepare reports. Refuse to allow yourself to become a *Deal Manager*.

158

Don't be a victim of the stereotypical sales persona. Avoid cigarette smoking and excessive alcohol consumption. Both vices are easily accessible at most sales-related gatherings, sometimes even free. However, each of them is proven to have negative effects on both your physical health as well as your sales fitness. The wise move is to avoid them altogether.

159

Employers – If you utilize a team of salespeople to promote and sell your product or service, join a trade group that can provide you with an annual compensation survey to ensure you have an industry-leading pay plan for them. It will make it much easier to attract AND retain the best talent…and having a happy, tenured sales team is a key driver of long-term market success!

160

One of, if not the first criteria in determining whether or not to move forward with a new project, idea, or offering, should be whether or not someone else in the basket of competitors is already doing it. If there isn't anyone, that's usually my cue to advance to the next step. If differentiation is one of your primary goals, and it should be, then any offering which is unique and exclusive to you sets the proper foundation for promoting the project. The next step is to determine what value that differentiation brings to your customer.

161

Thank You cards and Christmas gifts still work well as two components of an overall program for maintaining customer relationships. Just make sure they are unique, personalized, and of high-quality.

162

Byron McKenzie was a supplier sales representative I regularly purchased product from nearly two decades ago. As a *Thank You* for the orders I sent his way, Byron would periodically buy me dinner. He did that several times in the 2-3 years we did business together, before he was blessed to enjoy an early retirement. The funny thing is, Byron never attended a single one of those dinners. Instead, he would call me up from time to time and insist I take my wife out somewhere very nice and then send him the receipt. I've always thought that was pretty cool, and I still fondly remember him for it. No one else I've done business with has offered anything similar before or since. I don't need them to, and it's not a criterion in determining who I do business with, but it does confirm there are still plenty of ways for you to separate yourself from the crowd of competitors.

163

What happens when you have a pleasant and satisfying sales experience? You may mention it to a close friend or family member, and usually near the time of the transaction. What happens when you have a horrible, unsatisfying sales experience? You tend to remember it for decades and tell the story of it over and over when situations or circumstances trigger the memory. Make sure your efforts are remembered for being the pleasant and satisfying type.

164

Follow the LinkedIn *Company* pages of all your customers who have one. Then, through the Admin Panel on your own *Company* page, send invitations to *Follow* your page to all of your relevant individual first-level connections. This is a great practice for maintaining visibility and connectivity with influencers and decision makers.

165

The metaphorical concept of "Milking your own cows" is alive and well in the world of commerce. The greatest source of future sales resides with the customers you are already doing business with. When comparing the two, there will almost always be greater value in gaining a deeper connection with a current customer versus adding a new one.

166

Sales discussions go better when you can get your customers away from their office, or wherever it is they engage in their daily business routines. There tends to be less distractions, less opportunities to lose focus on the discussion at hand, and better retention of the content you cover. Knowing this, try to schedule *off site* meetings whenever possible.

167

Be mindful of the importance of tailoring your sales message to your audience. This is something I had to painfully learn as a young sales representative. For example, you wouldn't want to suggest, in the spirit of fairness, you be allowed to hold the same profit percentage in the sale of your product as your potential customer does in his, would you? What if I told you the customer happens to sell a product high in volume but with razor-thin margins?...asking for a friend.

168

There is another aspect to sales and selling which seems to be somewhat of a universal, yet informal law. That is, the larger the deal… the longer the customer's buying cycle and the more complex the requirements. My biggest *win* as a sales professional came exactly two years to the day from when my team and I had our first engagement with the customer's Supplier Development group. Patience is a virtue well-respected and often well-rewarded in the world of sales.

169

Gut check – Leaving your business card and a product brochure at the front desk does not qualify as a sales call. Unless you have a meaningful conversation with a decision maker, nothing really happened.

170

Keep a record of every sales presentation you've ever produced. They become great reference tools, they're cool for nostalgia purposes in seeing how your *pitch* has evolved over time, and sometimes you just plain forget things and need a reminder. For me, a best practice has been to keep a Dropbox account and permanently store everything in the *cloud*.

171

Most people have a desire to be helpful. When reaching out to a potential customer for the first time, preface your conversation with asking the individual for help. This will often cause defenses to come down and allow for a productive dialogue to begin. I recommend this strategy only on the initial contact, since in that case, the request should always be legitimate, and would thus be keeping with the requirements of honesty and authenticity ALWAYS.

172

I grew up in Southern California in the 70's and early 80's. Back then, Shakey's Pizza was an institution...and they're still around today. I remember seeing a sign behind the cash register which read, *"Shakey has no quarrel with those who sell for less. They know exactly what their product is worth."* It's generic in its focus and is a simple and effective challenge which can easily be adapted to whatever YOU are selling. Perhaps that was the genesis of my interest in sales strategy and argumentation. What was yours?

173

Take special care not to fall into the *Commodity Trap*. Years ago, at a financial reporting conference I attended, we got to the place in the agenda where we were discussing the anemic profit contribution levels of New Equipment Sales vs. the quite healthy levels from Parts and Service. It was at this point a sales management colleague named Carl stood up and loudly proclaimed, *"Look, everyone in this room knows…you have to give away the razors in order to sell the razor blades."* While the rest of us were sitting in stunned silence at the brash statement, another participant yelled out from the back of the room, *"Then why do they need you, Carl?!"* Enough said.

174

You will often hear the phrase, *"Sales is a relationship business"*. While true, many parrot the phrase without really giving much thought to it. One of the best sales reps I've ever hired once told me, while he would never admit it to his peers, any time his territory had been reduced…he had done better. He obviously knew the power of relationship, how to effectively leverage it, and the value of physically spending a greater amount of time with a smaller group of clients, current or potential. You would be wise to recognize the same.

175

When asking someone to choose between a range of options, i.e. A,B,C or D - 1,2,3, or 4 etc., most of us tend to pick the last choice presented. I'm sure there is some psychological explanation for that, but just file that away for now and add it to your mental database of human behavior.

176

Every year that goes by, differentiation at the product level becomes more difficult. There's always someone else in the market offering something similar or introducing a new feature or enhancement. Reviewing existing offerings for revision and improvement should be part of the regular activities of the product development team. Never let what you're selling become a victim of stagnation. Relevancy and currency are your friends.

177

When you reach the stage in the customer's buying cycle where they begin evaluating alternative suppliers, it's a good idea to develop some *Power Positions* in support of your value proposition. You may know them as Unique Selling Points (USPs), or perhaps in a more basic sense, as competitive advantages. Whichever term you use, you'll want to be sure they are reflective of items or aspects which are important to your customer, are unique to you, and are defensible and provable.

178

From microprocessors to industrial machinery, if you're selling a product which requires periodic maintenance to stay running at optimal levels, it likely has what accountants refer to as an *Economic Useful Life*. A product's EUL is exceeded when it becomes less expensive to acquire a new one vs. keeping and maintaining the existing one. We used to jokingly say the best time to replace your widget is the day before a catastrophic failure causes the EUL to immediately expire. HA, HA, HA, everyone in the sales presentation would laugh because, of course, no one could possibly know which day that would be. Guess what? With the advent of telematics, smart sensors, and big data, being able to pinpoint that fateful day is quickly becoming a real possibility. It doesn't matter WHAT you are selling…utilize technology as a differentiator and you will win more often.

179

You've likely heard the biblical phrase "Iron sharpens iron". What it means is that wise people should be questioning, encouraging, coaching, and challenging each other. Here's the charge - Make at least two friends in *Sales*. One who sells the same or similar thing you do, and to the same or similar industry, and another who sells something completely different to an unrelated market. Meet regularly as a group and share your successes and failures. The three of you will come up with so many ideas for each other, it will likely end up being the greatest growth accelerator you have.

180

Are you a sales *Lone Ranger*? Do you work remotely and with a great deal of autonomy? Remember this - with great freedom comes great responsibility. Never abuse your privileges of independence. The expectation is that you have the discipline to wisely manage your working hours. Never give anyone reason to doubt or question that.

181

Some may argue that absolute truth does not exist, and that knowledge regarding many factual claims is impossible. In philosophy, the latter is known as epistemological skepticism. What does all of this have to do with sales? There is something we know for certain about the external world to which there is no refute, and that is…there are NO new objections in sales, and NONE of those that exist should ever take you by surprise. Now…go do your homework.

182

Self-care is a practice which has received much more attention in recent years and taking an active role in protecting one's own well-being is increasing in popularity. Surround yourself with people who will love, support, encourage, and pray for you. *Safe spaces* should not be necessary, but a strong support network is a healthy, human requirement today.

183

There's a tendency for high-performing salespeople to be offered promotions to sales management. If you're one of those candidates, think carefully before gleefully jumping at the opportunity. The things which make you great with customers, might not necessarily make you a great manager of people. Secondly, much of what you enjoy about the sales profession could possibly be replaced with minutiae, bureaucracy, and politics. Lastly, you will likely give up some control over your compensation and become more dependent on others…proceed with caution.

184

The more you read, train, learn, interact with fellow professionals, and grow in your career, the larger your mental library of pithy quotes, wise sayings, insightful anecdotes, and sound advice will grow. *"Trust, but Verify"* is one of those, which I originally heard proclaimed by Ronald Reagan, and is a principle you would do well to employ regularly as you advance in your sales career.

185

Be careful not to run with the wrong crowd. There exists among most of us, an unconscious tendency to emulate certain behaviors of those we hang around the most. Even if we don't adopt any of the more questionable behaviors of some in our *crew*, others may attribute them to us due to the proximity and frequency of our association. To the extent possible, distance yourself from negative people, from those who love to hear themselves speak, and from individuals committed to self-promotion.

186

It's difficult for even the most highly trained orator to disguise when they are reading a script versus when they are speaking extemporaneously. For the rest of us who have had zero training, it's next to impossible. Once a potential customer discovers you are not speaking freely when making your pitch, your credibility is lost…never to be recovered. Avoid sales scripts like the plague. Better still, like COVID. Those who promote their use do not understand the selling process and should be ignored.

187

There's almost no greater job satisfaction than a customer you helped 20 years and a million miles ago, calling you out of the blue and asking for advice. A career in Sales can afford you many such moments of professional bliss.

188

ALWAYS consider the needs of others before your own. However, a servant attitude should never be employed with the goal of personal financial gain. Instead, it should be exercised out of a genuine love for others who have value, dignity, and worth…just like you.

189

From a career standpoint, never consider yourself *just* a salesperson. On the contrary, your role shoulders an immense responsibility for the health and strength of the entire enterprise. Remember, until something is sold, no one else in your organization has anything to work on. A sale is the genesis of all future corporate functions. Don't be intimidated by that…be heartened by the import of the part you play.

190

As previously prescribed, ALWAYS have a command of the features and benefits of your product or service. However, don't rely on those as the primary elements of your pitch. Maybe they will be seen as beneficial to your potential customer, but maybe not...and your competitor will have her own features and benefits which may be more appropriate for the problem your customer is trying to solve. Instead, focus the majority of your energy and effort on selling the OUTCOMES of owning or employing the product or service you are offering. Do this well and consistently and you will vault yourself into membership in your industry's sales elite.

191

Be careful about how you schedule your time off around the holidays. December can often be the biggest sales month of the year. To say it another way, some customers tend to be poor planners.

192

My wife thinks I'm absolutely nuts for finding enjoyment in them, but I say, learn to embrace and appreciate your airport, supermarket, and shopping mall experiences. Cultivating and nurturing a love of commerce can be inspirational for your selling activities.

193

If you generate and distribute sales proposals electronically, two things can make your life infinitely easier and will also separate you from many of your competitors…A high-resolution digital image of your handwritten signature, and a program which allows modification of PDF files (as of this writing, Adobe's Acrobat Pro is my personal preference).

194

If you have to drive clients around as part of your sales activities, be sure to have a clean, comfortable automobile with plenty of elbow room. A 5-year-old or newer vehicle is preferable.

195

Be someone who is always filled with optimism and enthusiasm! Let them become the attributes others immediately think of when someone mentions your name.

196

What's the best time to start talking to a potential customer about making a change from their current supplier and consider switching to you? Answer: Long before they need to. Most salespeople don't grasp how early in the buying process they need to start engaging their potential customer. In particular, if you represent a premium in the market, the need for early engagement is paramount. By the time the RFP comes out, it's usually too late to win. It's definitely too late to build the value necessary to justify your higher price.

197

Attention Sales Managers! - Don't buy books on Selling and give them to your team members, unless you have read them yourself, believe they are truly valuable, and can intelligently discuss the concepts and practices recommended therein. Just like we don't want the television to raise our children, throwing the latest sales philosophy du jour at your sales team, without thoughtful consideration, can often do more harm than good.

198

Business casual attire is generally accepted today for most information-gathering and pre-proposal sales discussions (Banking, Insurance, and Pharmaceutical products being the possible exceptions). But when it's time for the boardroom presentation, don't let your attire be inappropriate, disrespectful, or otherwise cause a distraction from the real subject of the meeting. Dress to impress!

199

"Everyone should be quick to listen, slow to speak, and slow to become angry"

- The Apostle James

…some of the best advice for today's sales professional.

200

It's important to have a creative outlet available during the non-working hours of your life. Regularly exercising your *Right Brain* can keep your sales creativity in top shape. Playing a musical instrument, painting, dancing, photography, pottery, martial arts, woodworking, or learning a foreign language are all great options.

201

Do you want a great conversation starter that works in almost any situation? Ask your potential customer where they grew up. This works particularly well if you happen to be well-traveled. A great runner-up to this question would be to ask your client how they happened to get into the business they are in.

202

Friendly Warning – Selling an invisible product like financing or insurance can be great for earning a healthy income and for continuously sharpening your selling skills, but at times can be difficult to maintain your excitement for. Conventional wisdom among those with selling experience in these fields say it's because you are not selling something you can put your hands on, or point to and say to yourself and others, *"This is what I do"*...just something to be aware of when selling intangibles.

203

Sales*men* - We don't usually make judgment calls based on each other's physical appearance. But when we do, the two areas of focus are generally our shoes and our wristwatch…be mindful of this…and prepare accordingly.

204

Make a BIG deal out of a NEW customer taking delivery of your product or service for the very first time. Put together a welcome package with a liberal amount of your branded swag. Include a personally signed letter of thanks from your CEO for joining your family of customers. If you are delivering and installing capital equipment, take a high-resolution digital photo of the customer and his employees gathered around the machine(s). Have it professionally framed along with a frame plate indicating the make and model and date of delivery. Encourage them to hang it in their front office. If you're delivering an intangible like software or a service, etc. do all of the above, but with everyone in a festive party pose in lieu of the equipment photo. Give them a commissioning experience like they've never had before. It will set the tone for a strong and long-term relationship.

205

What's the first thing you should do after the initial meeting with a potential new client? Find his profile on LinkedIn and send him a connection request. Second thing to do? Transfer 100% of the information on his business card into the Contacts app on your smartphone and then throw away the card. The customer contact data you gather during your career should remain with you until you retire.

206

If you still have a Fax number listed on your business card...get rid of it! Secondly, insist that your Marketing Department do the same for everyone in the company. There is perhaps no greater signal to your customers that you are either not evolving or not paying attention as an organization.

207

You want to make it easy for customers to do business with you? Great! Here's an easy lay-up for you…Be sure you accept the most popular form of commercial payment, the Credit Card, for whatever it is you sell. I don't care if it's $10 or $10M. If I can use a credit card to purchase a candy bar from a vending machine, a bag of peaches at a pop-up farmer's market, gas-station air for my slowly leaking front tire, or to pay a public parking meter, then I better darn well be able to purchase your product the exact same way. Are you worried about the 2-3% processing fee cutting into your profit margin? For starters, you should be perfectly willing to pay at least a portion of that for the convenience of immediate payment. For the remainder, just put an extra 1.5% into your deal and let your customer know you can accept his card as a payment alternative with no change in price. From a consumer standpoint, it's the safest form of payment. Don't deny your customer that option. Besides…some customers love to get the *miles.*

208

Unless you are employed in a hospital or work in the armed services, many business policies and practices are slow to evolve. Mistakes are tolerated and commitments to excellence are rare. This can have a profound impact on your sales success. Here's the prescription: Challenge the status quo. But do it with gentleness and respect…a practice which won't alienate you as a *complainer*.

209

Never implement a price increase unless you mean it. If a customer can call and get the increase removed or significantly reduced, you will have greatly damaged your credibility as a vendor. Future price increases, though perhaps necessary, will be more difficult to enact.

210

Attention Sales Managers! - Hire smart people, coach them to ensure their capabilities, empower them to execute your battle plan…then get out of their way. Give them autonomy and trust them to make their own decisions.

211

Make no mistake - Sales is a battle which you must prepare for. The quantity of competitors, the similarity among product offerings, and the intensity of pricing pressure are continuously increasing for EVERY industry. A passive and reactionary sales effort will get you nowhere…except looking for a different career.

212

If you have multiple levels of product/service offerings, i.e., Good - Better - Best, always start with your highest quality option (which should typically be your customer's best value). It's much easier to lessen a product offering, if necessary, than trying to move the customer *up* in price.

213

Seek to build relationships with your customers for altruistic reasons and not those of your pocketbook. The latter will be filled in proportion to the generosity of the former.

214

Customers will often tell you that purchase price is of great importance to them when evaluating alternative proposals. In reality, this is very rarely true. Is it a consideration? Sure. However, it is most often not the primary consideration, and in many cases is quite irrelevant depending on the type of product or service acquisition being contemplated. Consider the following:

"If the performance of the product affects the ability of the user to execute his or her task, price is the lowest priority."

\- Larry Steinmetz

215

Dropping your price is NOT the way to increase value. If the customer demands a concession, ADD something of worth instead, and just include it as part of your original offer.

216

When presenting a price, never be hesitant, nervous, timid, or reluctant in your actions. Instead, always make your offer with confidence and intentionality.

217

There are plenty of age-old proverbs related to the folly of those who speak loudly and often, as well as the wisdom of those who know when to hold their tongue or otherwise remain silent. In terms of verbal interactions, one truth is worth remembering…asking dumb questions will destroy your credibility as a sales professional.

218

Are you in the *Service* business, or do you have a service/support component to your product? Chances are your customer invoices are riddled with one or more of a litany of line items such as callout fee, travel charge, fuel surcharge, disposal fee, miscellaneous, zone charge, incidentals, supplies, program fee, etc. GET RID OF THEM. Figure out your average costs and required mark up, work backwards, and charge an equivalent rate for your work, but with an ***Everything is Included*** feature. Your customers will LOVE you for it, you will have little or no arguments over invoices, and you will be perceived as offering a higher-value service at a fair price.

219

Saturdays & Sundays = NO WAKE-UP ALARMS!

You've been charging hard all week. Your body and your mind need their rest.

Stay balanced.

220

Be an Innovator, an Ideator, and a Creative Thinker. Never say to a customer, *"We can match whatever those guys are offering"*. If you do, the first thing you are acknowledging is that your competitor brought the solution and not you. Second, you've now relegated yourself to competing only on price…two horrible positions to be in. You now have to *sell* your way out of them. Good luck!

221

We live and sell in a world of recessions, inflation, extreme cyclicality, supply chain disruptions, and a disappearance of conventional wisdom. Do whatever is necessary to make accommodations for good customers when times are tough. Help them through to the other side and you will likely be securing customers for life!

222

As much as customers are the lifeblood of any company, they don't always know what's best for themselves. They often get hyper-focused on their own area of expertise and rely on YOU to be doing your homework and presenting them with avant-garde solutions. Remember the perspective of Steve Jobs when he said, *"A lot of times, people don't know what they want until you show it to them."* It's still considered a controversial statement, but there's a current of wisdom running through it worthy of consideration.

223

Attention Sales Managers! - You were likely a star sales performer prior to your current role. Refuse to get caught up in corporate bureaucracy or political positioning within your company, and don't keep secret those actions, behaviors, and principles which helped you personally succeed. Share them with your team! Teach them and model them to your people and empower them to reach the highest levels of personal achievement. It's your job!

224

When traveling for business, it's tempting to live large and eat extravagantly on your employer's dime. Don't do it. Never compromise your safety or comfort...but don't create cause for scrutiny either.

225

It's important not to overthink or unintentionally complicate certain selling processes. Interestingly, salespeople and customers often want the same things from each other; The Truth, Regular Communication, Transparency, and No Surprises.

226

Attention Sales Managers! - Just like you should give special attention to your highest volume customers, be sure to take care of the high performers on your team as well. Do something *cool* for them, like graduating them from your standard, boring business cards to custom minted business coins. I recommend 1.5″ - 1.75″ antique brass which have some weight to them. Email me if you want to see an example.

227

Protect your word and your reputation above all else. Every step in your career progression is built on the one that preceded. To the extent possible, limit your dependence on others to deliver on promises you've personally made.

228

Many non-technical industries are ripe for disruption, having operated in the same manner for decades or longer. Focus your selling efforts on bringing new and innovative ideas, challenging norms, and questioning historical modes of operation, and you are bound to uncover revolutionary solutions which could propel you to record sales performance.

229

Think twice about spending marketing dollars on Radio or Television advertising. Consider using those funds for tangible, personalized gifts for your customers instead. In an earlier life, while selling equipment to the construction industry, our marketing department spent roughly $50,000 on post-game radio advertising with our local NBA team, and with no system in place to capture response rate. In retrospect, we could have purchased high-quality denim and suede jackets (highly valued by our customer demographic) with our company logo and customers' names embroidered on them, for one thousand of our key clients. That was 20 years ago. We would still be getting residual impressions today had we done that instead.

230

If you have a natural talent for speaking to large audiences, great! If not, pick a relevant topic you are passionate about and know you're good at, and volunteer to make a presentation on it at your next sales training meeting or trade association get-together. If that scares you, then join a local Toastmasters International club and work on improving your skills in this area…along with expanding your professional network.

231

Introspection is a healthy process to engage in from time to time. Self-reflection lets you process what you've learned, and through self-awareness you are less prone to deviate from the course you are on when difficulties arise. Be trustworthy. Be a person of your word. Confidently rely on yourself to follow through on your commitments…by keeping 100% of the promises you make to yourself. As French author André Gide famously said, *"Be faithful to that which exists nowhere but in yourself – and thus make yourself indispensable."*

232

If your potential customer finally pulls the trigger while you happen to be on vacation, sick leave, out of the office, or otherwise unavailable, it shouldn't matter. Credit for a sale should never be contingent on your physical presence. If your employer doesn't have your back in that situation, go sell for someone else who will appreciate you and your efforts.

233

Think about the last time you had a significant customer service-related problem. If you're anything like me, you just do not have the time to deal with it. You probably wanted to speak to the person with the authority to resolve it, to know they listened and heard your complaint, and to see that it got corrected quickly. Pretty basic, right? It's the same for your customer. In the case of a customer dispute, address the conflict immediately and in-person. Do this consistently as a matter of course and you will rarely lose a customer.

234

Most industries you sell into will tend to be well-connected, and quite often, the key players and influencers in those industries will be very communicative with each other. The following is a critical prescription to maintain for long-term success…Never burn bridges with your employer OR your customer. Throughout your career you will be amazed how many times a previous friendship, business relationship, or acquaintance has influence on a prospective sale.

235

Do you think customers are primarily concerned about price? Are you worried there's not a large enough market for premium products? Consider this: The average corporate age of Mercedes-Benz, Rolex, Cartier, Hennessy, and Tiffany & Co. is 166 years! There are hundreds of other similar companies I could have used as examples. The point is this…None of them are market share leaders, but they all produce an excellent product, have customers that love them, and they sell at THEIR price.

236

Take special care not to create any barriers, physical or virtual, which might make it difficult for customers to connect with you. For decades, Caterpillar required new distributors to establish facilities in the geographic center of their assigned territories, so as to be easily accessible to the greatest number of potential customers. Today, Caterpillar is the third most recognized brand in the world. Coincidence?

237

If you sell a product or service that offers the possibility of return, cancellation, or exchange, make sure the process of returning, canceling, or exchanging is simple, fast, and free. Follow the lead of Nordstrom, Amazon, and Costco…iconic American retailers known for their incredible customer service.

238

The greatest salespeople also tend to be some of the greatest thinkers. Aerobic exercise, strong personal connections, caffeine, meditation, a nutrient-rich diet, and sleep all serve as stimulants of healthy brain activity. Be sure to partake in balanced portions of all of the above.

239

There needs to be balance between work, family, and leisure time, without a doubt. However, with the advent of the smartphone, there is also no reason your customer shouldn't be able to connect with you 24/7/365. That's just one of the concessions you need to be comfortable in making as a sales professional.

240

Be a person of conviction, but when in the company of customers, understand that vocalizing strongly held beliefs in the areas of politics, faith, and the environment can be deeply divisive. Proceed with caution.

241

Take a typing class and become skilled at keyboarding. The only thing handwritten in business is your signature, and then, only until it is digitally scanned. You will be surprised at how quickly this skill can be learned…and how highly you will come to value it. One semester at a junior college may be all you need to attain proficiency.

242

Be convenient. Be helpful. Be innovative. Be unique. Be a group of individuals that is passionate about delivering the same, with joy and excitement. Bottom line…make it easy and fun to do business with you and customers will keep coming back.

243

Return customer texts, calls, or emails as quickly as possible. When asked for information, specs, drawings, testimonials, presentations, etc. provide them expeditiously. Set the precedent for follow-through and responsiveness. Just be prepared that in the end, none of it may matter. You will likely find only 10-20% of customers will notice, appreciate, and reward the behavior… but it's still the right thing to do.

244

Don't wait on your marketing department to get a budget approved for a limited number of customer testimonials. You've got cinema-grade audio and video at your fingertips with your latest smartphone. Purchase a small, flexible phone tripod and you've got an instant studio. Set it up on their desk and start recording impromptu conversations with your customers. Get their permission to share them and you'll have one of the most powerful sales tools known to man.

245

Become an avid reader, a frequent traveler, and maintain an active social life. Success in selling often has a positive correlation to the breadth of your frame of reference. Regularly take in knowledge from every aspect of your life and lean on your experiences for connection and relatability.

246

If you're a believer that your word is your bond, then treat your sales proposal in the same manner. There should be no allowance for deviation from the pricing and promises set forth in your customer quote. P.S. – demand the same from your own vendors.

247

Years ago, I hired branding guru and customer service expert, Joe Calloway, to lead an off-site training session for our sales team. He exhorted us to not simply be one or two steps ahead of our competition, but to elevate customer expectations by working in such a manner as to create an entirely new category of company, exclusive to us. We had never thought about or approached our business in such a manner prior to this point. It was refreshing and transformative, and ultimately provided the building blocks for us to make a leap in our evolution as a sales force. The prescription...Don't rely solely on internal experience and expertise as you journey on your path of continuous improvement. Whether individually or corporately, bring in resources from outside the organization from time to time to help examine and critique what you do from an entirely different perspective. Thanks Joe!

248

Often times the bright, shiny, super cool features or technologies that help secure the sale, fail to get implemented or utilized through some sort of incomplete set-up or activation during the product commissioning process. Be sure you have rock solid, process-mapped delivery procedures which ensure your customer receives EXACTLY what was sold.

249

Set a future activity in your CRM software to meet with your client 1-2 months before their warranty, service agreement, or tech support expires. While there, conduct a courtesy examination of your product or service and see if there might be any issues which can be resolved prior to expiration. A few things will happen as a result; They will be blown away by your proactive service, you will many times uncover a need for additional features or options, and best of all, they will know you have their back. That's just part of premium service and is something they will tell their friends, customers, and business acquaintances about.

250

Although it somewhat depends on the type of product you sell, not many customer visits to your facility are family affairs. Perhaps more often they should be. If a client ever comes to visit you with one of their young children in-tow, make sure that kid ALWAYS takes home a toy. Your receptionist should have age-specific novelties at-the-ready. Do something cool for your client's children and you'll have a customer for life.

251

Computers, automation, artificial intelligence, and general technological advancement have been making our lives much easier in so many ways. But not so much in the area of customer service. If you have any type of automated phone attendant system in use during regular business hours…turn it off. There is still NO adequate substitute for live, friendly, helpful, and personal service.

252

Spend more time in revenue-generating activity and less time in non-revenue generating activity. If you don't know off the top of your head which is which, sit down and chart it out. You will likely be surprised you've ever made a dime.

253

No matter how great you think your carefully crafted pitch or subject heading may be, never send unsolicited prospecting emails. It's one of the biggest wastes of time on the planet… and makes you look desperate.

254

Patronization is possibly the most off-putting behavior that can be directed toward a potential customer. Shockingly, it's still promoted in a number of mediums as a valid starting point for a variety of sales discussions…"*so how's your day goin'?*"

255

Certain personal physical attributes are unconsciously held in high regard. The most famous and oft studied being height. Bottom line, taller people tend to be more successful and receive greater compensation than their vertically challenged colleagues. If you're a man over 6′ tall or a woman taller than 5′7″, exploit this psychological preference to your advantage. Combine it with a sense of humor and a knack for small talk and you'll be unstoppable. I once had a team member…we'll call him Steve. Steve was 7′1″, gregarious, and never at a loss for words. Making sales calls with him was mesmerizing. I was convinced we could cold-call the Pentagon and get in to see whomever we wanted.

256

Another phenomenon of psychological preference is eyeglasses. People who wear them are somehow perceived as being more intelligent and better educated than those who don't. There's not much you can do about your height, but ANY pair of eyeglass frames can be ordered with clear, non-prescription lenses. So, if we're building the ideal physical profile for sales success, it would be 2+ inches taller than average, sharp dresser, glasses, well-spoken, well-traveled, confident, and witty.

257

Do we really need any more books on sales? Aren't there other, more important aspects of business and commerce which are critical to learn and understand? Unless you are employed in the trade, you probably haven't given much thought to the fact we're ALL in sales. Selling is about influencing others, and that's pretty much everything we do... everywhere...every day.

258

If a potential customer says, *"Oh Wow! I didn't know that was possible"* or *"I didn't realize we could do that"*, be encouraged and know you're on the right track.

259

Never underestimate the power of the internet and how it has radically reshaped the buying cycle and selling processes. Research shows that for many products, fully 80% of prospective clients have already done some type of online investigation into what they're looking for before they ever contact you. Knowing this...be thoughtful, intentional, and strategic in how you position yourself, your company, and your product or service on the World Wide Web.

260

As disappointing as it is to acknowledge, we have reached a point in our society where even a rudimentary level of customer service skill stands out from the crowd. Be a student of every transaction you're a party to, e.g., at the bank, the supermarket, the cell phone store, the fast-food establishment, Starbucks, etc. You will readily experience both right and wrong ways to deliver service. Learn from those experiences. I was once successful in obtaining a regional sales management role for a manufacturer because I proved I knew exactly how NOT to treat my customers. That was a refreshing perspective for the hiring manager.

261

Interpreting Body Language is another discipline super helpful to salespeople, the study of which has advanced significantly in recent years. Sign up for a course at your local community college and prepare to be blown away. Remember too, you can speak volumes to people before you ever open your mouth. St. Francis of Assisi appeared to be prescient in this regard when he famously said, *"Preach the gospel at all times and if necessary, use words."*

262

Many of the most successful salespeople I have had the pleasure of working alongside, started their careers in a technical area of their industry or field. Some of them never had sales aspirations, but eventually came to discover that a thorough understanding of how their product worked, and being able to clearly articulate such to customers, was a powerful tool for sales success…and it still is.

263

The longer I progress in my sales career, the more transparent I have become in my approach with potential customers. Give them a certain measure of behind-the-scenes insight into your business and your industry and they will feel empowered. You will also have assisted in giving them a bit of an upper hand when engaging alternative suppliers. Either way, if you play it correctly, you will quickly be seen as their advocate and respected as a straight shooter. This has worked well for me and has strengthened my personal brand without bringing any detrimental exposure to my employer.

264

I once interviewed a couple of up-and-coming sales reps in Southern California who asked me what my office requirement was. When I asked them to clarify the question, they revealed to me their current employer required the field sales team to be at their desks at 8:00 am every morning…how ridiculous, I thought. My answer to them was that I preferred they be having breakfast with their customer at that time instead, and there would be no "office requirement" if they came on board.

265

As many of today's sales influencers have rightly pointed out, Cold Calling as a sales generation strategy is dead. Unless you're peddling World's Finest Chocolate bars for your child's school fundraiser, don't waste your time. You're just doing it to collect names you say? OK, but this is the post-information age we're living in. I can get 10X the number of decision makers' names in a quarter of the time, without leaving my office. You should be able to do the same.

266

Never use the word "can't" in a sales dialogue with a customer. This will require some grammatical skills, but always frame your conversations in such a way that you only ever discuss what you CAN and are enthusiastically WILLING to do for your potential client. I have to give credit here to my friend and mentor, Julio Herrera Leos, who coined the phrase, *"Don't tell me Why No, tell me How Yes." Como Si,* right Julio?

267

It's important to take a keen interest in your customer's business. You will typically be bringing an outside perspective and a fresh set of eyes. Your skills will take some time to develop, but the results are worth the effort. Uncover a problem your customer has not yet discovered on his own, pair it with a solution only you can provide, and guess what…an iron wall will have just gone up in front of your competition.

268

The interconnectivity, both virtual and physical, of suppliers, distributors, end-users, and third-party reviewers is providing customers with more data than ever when entering the research phase of their buying cycle. Product brochures, spec sheets, YouTube demonstration videos, customer testimonials, and user reviews being available online often takes away your mystique or "Wow" factor by the time the initial customer meeting occurs. If you haven't established a relationship and a dialogue prior to this phase, you may be faced with, *"We know exactly what we want, what do you guys charge for it?"* If that's happening with your opportunities more than 50% of the time, it could be an indication you are not engaging potential customers early enough. Keep reading and keep this book in your sales toolbox for reference.

269

Join a Business Networking group in the city in which you live or work, or one in each. There are loads of them. Most of the time they have membership limitations relative to industry representation so that you are never in the same room with your arch nemesis, and so that group members can achieve maximum networking benefit with each other. This will require time and commitment outside of traditional working hours. But you've likely already come to the understanding this is a necessary requirement for continual progression in your career.

270

We've all enjoyed hearing stories since we were kids. Stories from distant uncles, camp counselors, best friends, and quirky neighbors have often been some of the best. Your customers are no different. Present them with a riveting or interesting story of your company's history, a customer's user experience, or plans for future product development, and you've got their attention. I've touched on a few personal attributes of great salespeople in this book. Being a dynamic and compelling storyteller should be among them.

271

The old joke that goes, *"You know the best way to get rid of a salesperson?...buy something from them"* is sadly, often true. Never let yourself be the butt of that joke. Instead of just selling your stuff and moving on to the next customer, sell outcomes which are new, and an improvement for your client, and don't let your commission check be the end of the process. Let it signify the beginning of a long-term, value-driven, loyal relationship.

272

Never process a credit, grant a concession, or apply a discount behind the scenes. Send a revised invoice or issue a new account statement which clearly shows the reduction. You always want to ensure you are receiving both visibility and credit for any goodwill you are extending to your customer. It's one of the elements which helps create loyalty and which solidifies relationships.

273

"So, where do I start?" I get this question from many brand-new salespeople. Here's how you begin: Schedule visits with each of your existing customers (anyone in your territory that has bought something from your company in the last 5 years). Introduce yourself, tell them the story of how you got to be sitting in front of them, inform them of your desire to help, and ask how you can position yourself to be the best business partner for them today, and going forward. No matter what you're selling, the goal should be to assist in improving your customer's productivity, profitability, or both.

274

When managing a geographic sales territory, a few core practices can be helpful. 1. When planning a route of customer visits, travel to the furthest point first. 2. If you sell to multiple industries, segment them and focus on one at a time. 3. Overlay your existing customers onto a map. Look for geographic gaps. If there is no valid reason for a lack of customers in those areas, devise a game plan to fill them in with new clients. 4. It's best to develop these "target" account plans alongside other stakeholders in the company. Make it a team effort.

275

Want to achieve a steady income even though a large component of your compensation is commission? Keep the right balance of early-stage lead qualification, mid-stage opportunity development activity, and late-stage proposal presentations. You or your sales director may use alternate terms, but what we're talking about here is called sales funnel management. In conventional parlance, don't just be an elephant hunter or swinging for the Home Run…be sure to get plenty of base hits along the way.

276

The line between a proper level of prompting, and applying too much pressure for your customer to act is a fine one. It's often best navigated through creating an indirect sense of urgency. For example, creatively and subtly allowing your customer to discover you have numerous colleagues competing for sales of the same item(s), or that there is a limited amount of inventory which is quickly diminishing. Also, letting your customer know there are scheduled price increases which could become effective any day, or that there are rising supply constraints which are soon going to make the product more difficult to obtain. These are all ways to effectively create urgency. There could be many others in your business, but whatever they are, they must always be truthful. DO NOT fabricate these or any others simply to create a false sense of urgency.

277

Here is an ever-present certainty to always be mindful of as a salesperson: The *truth* never stays hidden forever…and will eventually be revealed.

278

In rare instances, performance comparisons can be a tool for self-improvement. More often they serve to damage self-confidence and overall mental health. Don't compare, benchmark, or otherwise gauge your level of success against others. Focus instead on achieving, then beating your own *Personal Bests*. Work on continuously becoming a better version of yourself and sell in such a way that YOU are your biggest competitor and no one else.

279

Live generously. Consider others' needs before your own. Always ask how you can help. Be kind.

280

Take a page out of the Southwest Airlines playbook. They have been consistently profitable year after year in a tremendously volatile and competitive industry. How do they do it? Among other things, they figured out a way to simplify the complex, they focus on their strengths and what they are naturally good at, they standardize processes to eliminate waste and prevent bureaucracy, and as everyone who has flown them knows… they are friendly and fun to be around. Sounds like a recipe for sales success if I've ever heard one.

281

As I have pointed out earlier, stellar customer service is the secret to long-term sales success. Consistently support your product at a level the customer has never experienced before, and future sales are virtually guaranteed. I once nervously presented a new offer to a current customer after several price increases and service labor rate hikes since his previous purchase 5 years earlier. At the boardroom table, the CEO immediately flipped to the last page of the proposal. The price page! Expecting the worst, I was surprised as he quickly asked if *Gary* would remain as his service technician. Assuring him of the same, he swiftly replied, *"Where do I sign?"* To this day, it was the easiest sale of my career…and not because of anything I or my sales team had done. If you're taking care of customers the right way, like *Gary* was, EVERY sale can be that easy.

282

When speaking to potential customers about your company, your product, or your service, always hold and present each in the highest regard. You should be using *Industry Standard, the authority, reference standard, industry benchmark* and other such descriptive terms in your speech.

283

Differentiation is mentioned several times in this book. That's because it's important. But just being different is pointless, unless that difference brings value to your customer and makes your solution the better alternative. So, strive for differentiation, absolutely…but with the goal of process and product improvement and not simply competitive separation.

284

Yet another reason for committing to stand behind the terms set forth in your proposal is the legal doctrine known as *Detrimental Reliance*. If in the course of commercial trade, your customer relies on his acceptance of your proposal to subsequently make binding business decisions of his own, he may have recourse for any change in your terms which could then pose a detriment to his business. You would have to consult an attorney to be sure, but it's best to just be a man or woman of your word.

285

I've got volumes of responses to various sales objections which I've archived over the years, some of which are universal in application, but many being quite subjective and dependent on the audience and my relationship with them. Honing your social intelligence skills to know exactly when and to whom you can use a particular response is a powerful sales differentiator. For an example of this, see *Don Draper's* response to his potential client when pitching an advertising campaign for Bel Joli lipstick in AMC's *Mad Men*, episode 39.

286

Build a virtual moat around your customer which makes them impenetrable by the competition. How do you do that? By partnering with them and becoming integral to their business and how they go to market. What does that look like? As an example, I've had customers call me from time to time and ask if I would allow them to provide a workspace in their facility for one of my team members. My answer..."*ABSOLUTELY!*"

287

If or when you change industries in your career journey, seize the opportunity to maintain an outsider's perspective in your new gig. When launching into a new venture, you bring with you the advantage of not having been caught up in the behavioral and procedural norms of your new employer. It's often the period where you ask the most *Why* questions. My challenge for you is to never stop asking *"Why?"* Never let yourself become the one who says, *"Well, because this is the way we've always done it."*

288

Commit yourself to always representing a premium brand and product. You'll have way more fun, make lots more money, and have a ton of opportunities for growth and advancement during your career. Those who are more comfortable representing a lesser product, and selling on price, tend to have careers marked by stagnation and mediocrity.

289

A sales role is not typically a salaried position. Budgeting for fluctuations in your personal income is a wise practice for most salespeople. A percentage for charity, a percentage for savings, and the balance for *living* is a popular model. As an overarching principle, always spend less than you make. Do that for a really long time and you will have much less to worry about as you get older.

290

Make the decision to get a dog. Don't be afraid to spend the money on getting a healthy, well-tempered one from a reputable breeder. People who have dogs tend to live longer, have lower blood pressure, are more socially adept, and are more often purpose-driven and creative. Plus, it adds another facet to your frame of reference when establishing rapport and conversing with potential customers.

291

WORK HARD…PLAY HARD…SLEEP HARD. In that order.

292

Be a student of your trade. Study and analyze your industry, your competitors, your product, and your customers. Take an intellectual approach. Search the internet for relevant research papers and read what others have discovered through investigation. For a professional sports analogy, the Hall of Fame inductees tend to be the ones who, in the early morning hours, spend precious time reviewing game tape and taking notes to improve their mental and physical skillsets.

293

Vive la différence as the French would say. While this common phrase is rarely made in reference to variation among tangible consumer products, it is indicative of the growing value of diversity in general. The level of product differentiation vis-à-vis your competitor is directly proportional to the additional premium you can justify, but ONLY when that differentiation results in added value for your customer.

294

In sales, there is no substitute for time spent on the frontline with customers. This is where everything happens. This is where you keep current on industry trends. This is where you hone your skills in personal interactions. This is where you stay sharp on questions, answers, challenges, and refutations. This is where deals are done and relationships are built. This is where you need to spend as much of your time as possible.

295

All of your selling efforts, post-sale support efforts, relationship-strengthening efforts, and consultative recommendations should be viewed figuratively as wrapping your arms around your customer. What happens then? Your customer feels loved, appreciated, safe, confident, and empowered.

296

Marketing expert and author Kerry Bodine says, *"Exceptional customer experiences are the only sustainable platform for competitive differentiation."* Remember this truth, and adopt it as one of the principles which will guide your selling efforts.

297

If memory serves, my remote sales communication evolution was pay phone - pager - bag/trunk phone - basic handheld phone - more advanced handheld phone - fat flip phone - Nextel - Blackberry - Skinny flip phone - iPhone. Oh, and a Palm Pilot or two in there somewhere. Are your selling skills continuously evolving in the same manner? They should be. If you're getting new phones more often than new customers…there's a problem.

298

It's difficult to justify the exorbitant cost of exhibiting that has become the standard fare of the modern Trade Show. Participation is commonly assumed to have little or no effect on long-term sales order volume. Customers typically do not choose business partners or make purchasing decisions based on whether or not the supplier had a booth at the last exhibition. Almost universally, exhibitors agree the money spent could have been utilized more effectively elsewhere. At the same time, the conclusion is generally the same...we GOTTA be in the show! It continues to be a sales phenomenon.

299

This will seem contraindicative to most, but be careful when desiring 100% of your customer's business. Performance expectations will be greater, pricing pressure higher, and your status as sole supplier will be continuously scrutinized. My friend Cliff never wants to be his customer's primary supplier. He wants to be their secondary supplier. In his words, *"Sooner or later my competitor is going to make a promise they won't be able to keep, and I'll be there to save the day and be the hero. Eventually, I'll end up getting all of their business without having to ask for it"*. Apparently, this pattern interrupt of wanting to be the back-up quarterback and not the starter, is working...Cliff is gaining more customers than ever before.

300

Quiet Quitting was invented by customers decades ago, and long before anyone put a name to it. When a customer leaves you for the competition, lets their service contract expire, or decides to buy someone else's widget, they usually do so quietly and without notification. For you parents, the analogy of children fits perfectly here. When you know they're not sleeping, but you haven't heard a peep out of them for several minutes...it's usually bad news.

301

My wife recently registered for, and attended a sales webinar from a highly respected, nationally known financial advisor. At the end of the presentation a discount was offered for the advertised training program, BUT they only had room for 36 participants! Her response? *"Immediately, NO!"*. Never insult the intelligence of your audience…especially not with a grade-school gimmick.

302

The popular cautionary adage regarding making assumptions is especially valid in the discipline of selling. Never assume, simply because your mission statement mentions it, that you know exactly what your customer's expectations are. The breakneck speed of business, ushered in by online retailers and next-day delivery companies, implicitly burdens you with an aggressive delivery expectation…warranted or not. Always clarify the expected terms of performance when finalizing your deal.

303

For many industries, there's a flurry of sales activity near the end of the calendar year. Remaining budget dollars have to be spent, tax incentives and deductions need to be secured, and purchases are often made prior to anticipated price increases. Be mindful that this is also Holiday season. To the extent possible, conclude the year's business by the 15th of December. The remaining two weeks are completely unpredictable.

304

Is the product you sell often leased or financed? Pro Tip: Get all financial documentation executed by the required principals at or near the time of order. Once delivery occurs, generally any employee can sign the Delivery & Acceptance form. Your complete doc package can then immediately be submitted to your lender for funding…which is when you get paid, right? Waiting to coordinate signatures at product commissioning and hoping all necessary parties are on site, just invites delays. Don't make that rookie mistake.

305

As much as I loathe the New Automobile buying experience, and marvel at the industry's lack of evolution in sales approach, the one thing they often get right is *Delivery*. Don't subsequently sabotage the value you've created with your customer by offering a lackluster delivery experience. Invite all appropriate customer representatives, install and commission your product with fanfare and excitement, and give the customer a delivery moment the likes of which they have never experienced prior.

306

Certain human interactions have the ability to more frequently influence behavior in others. Physical touch, the volume and pace of speaking, and facial expressions are just a few examples. One basic physical interplay to be conscious of in your selling efforts is eye contact. Whether speaking, listening, or shaking hands, maintaining eye contact with your customer can be influentially powerful.

307

Most traditional descriptions of the *Steps of a Sale* begin with *Establish Rapport,* or something similar. The reason is, having the potential customer *like* you or at least feel comfortable conversing with you, is the prerequisite to moving forward in the process. This is the case no matter where in the world you are selling, as this truth transcends cultures, ethnicities, and personalities. Take some time to learn basic greetings and salutations in several different languages. It's often a great ice breaker and conversation starter when meeting with customers whose native language is different than your own.

308

In sales, as in most occupations, there are trends, changes, and evolutions which occur over time. This is why it will always be impossible to learn everything there is to know about the selling trade. The necessity of lifelong learning is inevitable. Be proactive and intentional about staying current, skilled, and relevant in a dynamic marketplace.

309

Believe it or not, certain customers still expect, and sometimes abuse, the offer of dining, entertainment, or gifts from their vendors. It's rare, but it occasionally happens. Politely decline any requests to visit adult clubs, bars, or other questionable venues. That's not a behavior you want to cultivate, and it may be indicative of a customer relationship you want to avoid.

310

There's something to be said for representing boutique firms. The larger the enterprise, the more difficult to maintain the founding vision and to keep everyone on mission. Do your research when selecting who you want to represent in the marketplace. Look for an organization where everyone in the company is committed to supporting the Sales Department.

311

Before he and I ever became friends, I brought my wife's car to Bill for a routine oil change at his auto repair facility in the small town where we lived in Northern California. Upon picking it up, Bill apologized profusely for accidentally triggering the *Check Engine* light. Although it created no mechanical issues, and he had a plan for correcting it in a few days, he refused to charge me anything for the service he performed. I argued that the free service was not necessary, but he insisted. I immediately thought to myself, if he is compelled to take responsibility for something so minor, I can trust him with ANYTHING related to my family's automobiles. I've referred numerous customers to him since and have been re-telling this story for 20 years…all for what likely cost him about $15 in parts!

See #143.

312

My wife received a random and unsolicited text from a home improvement contractor we had worked with several months earlier. He was reaching out to say his wife was a freelance photographer, was booking appointments for holiday photos, and wanted to know if we were interested. It felt to her like an intrusion, a violation of privacy, and an abuse of a previous acquaintanceship. The subsequent phone call after her non-response was the final nail in his coffin. His proxy solicitation of clients on behalf of his wife's business wreaked of desperation. The prescription is this...Never exploit a customer relationship for something that wasn't intended or requested.

313

Pay for a membership to your local library. If it's a decent one, they will have a reference section with the ability to access numerous online databases through your paid enrollment. There is a wealth of highly detailed information you can drill down on for almost any industry and company type you can think of. This has proven to be one of the best ways to identify and target potential customers, and to conduct pre-call research.

314

The level of control our portable electronic devices have over us often borders on the unhealthy. The compulsion to *check* them while in the company of others can be seen as rude, inattentive, or both. Switch your smartphone to vibrate, or if you have the courage, turn it off altogether when in customer meetings, sales training, performance reviews, job interviews, or family mealtime.

315

Success in selling is often about bringing the best solution to what the customer has determined is a problem or pain point. Consider the wisdom of Franciscan friar, William of Ockham. His well-known philosophical principle, Ockham's Razor, advocates for the simplest solution to a problem as most often being the correct one. Try using that as a starting point when formulating your offer.

316

In the case of a customer dispute, always offer a credit before agreeing to a refund. A refund of $3000 will cost you $3000. A credit of $3000, which can be used to purchase something you offer with a 50% margin, would only cost you $1500! All the while, the value to your customer remains constant. That's not deceptive…that's just smart business.

317

Trying to get your new sales career off the ground? Think about this...Maximum takeoff thrust for a modern commercial airliner is 70% - 80% greater than its cruising thrust. You should behave in a similar manner and attack every new endeavor at Full Throttle!

318

Even the BEST outbound lead generation service will never know your business or be able to make your pitch as well as you. There's no reason to hire a third-party provider for something you'll always be able to do more effectively and efficiently in-house.

319

Your ultimate goal as a sales professional is that, at a certain point in the future, 100% of your sales will be coming from Referral, Reputation, or Repeat business. It's not a task for the timid. Long hours and lots of hard work will be required to reach the end of that rainbow. Buckle up!

320

Never let an objection surprise you. Anticipate what the objection will likely be, have your best response(s) loaded into your memory bank ready to deliver, and condition yourself not to act alarmed. If the customer thinks they've got you rattled, they will tend to gravitate toward a more offensive posture, expecting you to offer up a concession. Play it calm and cool.

321

Use your life experiences and stories from activities outside of your work life to color your conversational style and customer approach. Being a *real* person that is neither consumed with work, nor checked out and apathetic, will be more relatable to the majority of your customer base.

322

You should never lament the fact you are not yet a sales superstar. Start where you are and with what you've got. Commit to learning something new every day. Learn from every win. Learn from every loss. Invest both time and resources into continuously improving your skills. Your rate of growth will generally be commensurate with the amount of your investment.

323

Salespeople are master justifiers…and masters of excuses. Some of the more common being, *"Business is Slow"…"It's getting near the holidays"…"There's an election coming up"…"Most of my customers are on vacation"… "There's not a lot of activity right now"*, etc. Don't waste time wishing the market was behaving differently, that circumstances were like they were in the past, or trying to justify your lack of initiative. Sales are happening every day no matter how much you think they're not, even during a pandemic or a recession…or when it's raining outside.

324

Attend seminars, webinars, and listen to motivational speakers, but remember this… the reason they can draw a crowd year after year is because they've been able to successfully craft a *Mountaintop Experience*. As such, they know 90% of the attendees will fall back into their regular pattern of behavior after only one week. Here's the fix: attend with one of your closest co-workers and then hold each other accountable for implementing the behaviors and improvements you got fired up about and know in your heart you should make.

325

Be generous in sharing the stories of your successes with your fellow team members. Someone shared theirs with you at some point, and we're all on a journey of continuous improvement. Reinforcing successful, profitable, and competent practices makes us better individually and also puts our profession in a better light.

326

There's no disputing the fact education opens doors. An undergraduate degree has been the minimum cost of entry into the business world for decades now, and a graduate degree has become the new expectation for those wishing to advance in their careers. The advent of the virtual classroom has made earning one more convenient than ever, and chances are, your employer may pay for most of it. It's no small commitment, but the gratifying sense of accomplishment and the increase in advancement opportunities are more than adequate justification.

Go get it!

327

Shun any games, gimmicks, or tricks in your efforts at influencing your customer to make a purchase. For example, asking your potential customer a series of questions that will only have *"Yes"* answers, then quickly following with a query regarding desire for your product in the hope of benefitting from verbal repetition. If you ever hear anyone advocating for that ridiculousness, cast out that sinner from among you!

328

Materialism is all around us, and monetary wealth is often promoted as the universal measure of success. The sales profession can certainly be very lucrative. However, financial gain should never be your sole motivation. You need to have a greater purpose that drives you. Those that do tend to be the wealthiest of all…and their bank accounts are healthy too.

329

The need for adaptation is not just necessary for physical life, but also for the life of your sales career. Stay teachable, coachable, open-minded, and inquisitive. Challenge status quo, embrace new technologies, don't take yourself too seriously, and always be willing to try something new.

330

Spend some time in each of the operational support areas of your company, e.g., Accounting, Marketing, Order Processing, Customer Service, etc. Shadow a fellow employee, offer to participate on a cross-functional team, or attend training courses for other departments. Having first-hand knowledge of how the entire enterprise functions will make you a better salesperson.

331

It's an erroneous assumption that you need to possess significant experience, education, or expertise in a given field or industry in order to be considered for a sales position there. To start, you just need to be intelligent, friendly, personable, and eager to learn. I worked with a very successful leader early in my banking career who had is undergraduate degree in Geology!

332

Each of us is wired differently. It can be both difficult and frustrating when trying to learn in a prescribed manner or to act in a particular way which we are innately unsuited for. Take a few personality and temperament tests. I can recommend TJTA, Enneagram, Myers-Briggs, and DISC. Learn what your natural strengths are and play to those strengths. It just may be that it will ALL start coming together for you.

333

Traveling, trade shows, customer visits, presentations, hot sunny days with lots of windshield time…they all take their toll in sapping your energy. Even so, pitching your product and presenting solutions for customers should instantly fire you up, no matter how long of a day it's been. If that's NOT the case for you, it could be indicative of your need for a change.

334

Whether leading a sales meeting, making a boardroom presentation, delivering a keynote address, or hosting a webinar, always start by putting your audience at ease. The best way to do that is through cleverly using humor. Healthy laughter releases both endorphins and dopamine which prepare your hearers mentally and physically to listen, consider, participate in, and retain what it is you are about to share.

335

"Give me a call if you have any questions" has to be the all-time worst example of a next-step commitment. It's actually a non-commitment. It's a reflection of complete disengagement from what you're trying to accomplish. It reveals a lack of thought and a lack of effort. Purge that phrase from your sales lexicon… and think more critically about what it is you are trying to achieve.

336

They say imitation is the sincerest form of flattery. It's also a surefire way to destroy your reputation as a solutions provider. There is no creativity and certainly no brainpower involved in agreeing to match whatever the *other guys* are offering. You have to be unique in your approach to the market, your product offering, and your execution. There is no tolerance for copycats in the business of selling. You may be sincere and think you are being helpful, but *"The road to hell is paved with good intentions"* has become a popular maxim for a reason.

337

Don't forget you are constantly being compared to others. As much as your mother told you it shouldn't be done, it happens every day in business. Even though you may be the only one providing your particular type of product or service, you're being compared against every other supplier your customer transacts with. Where do you think you'll be ranked? Are you sure? Check in with them at least once a year to find out how your supplier relationship is being perceived. Pivot wherever necessary if you don't occupy the top spot.

338

Attention Owners, Presidents, MDs, CEOs! - Certain elements of your Sales Department should be sacrosanct. As a young sales manager, a mentor cautioned me, *"You can't mess with people's pay."* Even today, I'm surprised at how many top performers are driven out of their organizations through constant pay plan modifications, commission limitations, and arbitrary compensation restrictions. Let me be clear. No one is immune from performance evaluation or critical review. But when it comes to compensation, figure out a fair plan, where sales compensation is commensurate with deal profitability, and then leave it alone!

339

Perhaps the most difficult word for a salesperson to hear is *"No"*. Sometimes just as difficult is to say the same to a potential customer. But that's exactly what you need to condition yourself to do, and learn to be OK with, if it's not a good fit. Too many potentially great business relationships have been prevented from developing because the salesperson made a premature promise and was awarded an obligation he would never be able to fulfill. Though temporarily painful, the wise path is to decline the opportunity until such time you have the capability to execute the way the customer expects.

340

Diversification is not just a popular investment strategy. Some of the most successful salespeople are those who can sell across multiple industries, who can creatively figure out new uses and applications for their products, and who pursue opportunities with both small and large customers alike. It's also a great tactic for maintaining performance consistency in times of economic downturn or market uncertainty.

341

The Marketing Department, Sales Department, Engineering, Service Department, Product Development, and Executive Teams all like to claim that commercial success is primarily dependent on THEM. So, who's right? All of them are. The key factor to profitable growth is the quality of the Customer Experience (CX). EVERY department and EVERY individual has both an opportunity and an obligation to contribute to the CX, and should be professionally trained on how to best do so.

342

The salesperson stereotype which some have grown to hate, is the *Old School* rep who sold through coercion, trying to create a sense of obligation to buy on the part of the purchaser. That methodology is dead, hopefully never to be resurrected. Today's informed salesperson understands the enjoyment a buyer gets from making a purchase and works to channel that desire toward their product. In the end, we all love to buy things, right? It's where the concept of *Retail Therapy* comes from. So then…generate enough excitement so that we all want to buy YOURS!

343

Develop and embrace the concept of vertical integration in your sales activities. For any single transaction, once you've been awarded the business, it is best to keep the number of suppliers, installers, departments, and individuals at the minimum necessary level. The more you can drive and control the various components of your deal internally and without dependence on others, the less chance of something going wrong and the greater the chance of delivering exactly what you promised in the exact time you estimated. In the end, your reputation is everything. Don't outsource it to others if you don't have to.

344

As contradictory as it may sound, learn to temper your enthusiasm a bit. When asked to develop a list of target accounts for the next year, too many of us are given to choosing a quantity not feasibly manageable. Take heart, it's more a sign of a passion for what you do than it is poor time management. Customer growth that is methodical, incremental, and which yields loyal, value-driven relationships, wins the day. Chasing after new customers in the pursuit of some arbitrary growth metric, while the customers leaving through the back door escape unnoticed, has become an all too prevalent paradox.

345

What would happen if you shifted your focus and attention from *New Customer Acquisition* to *Zero Customer Loss*? What would that look like? What would you start doing for your customers that you're not doing today? Shouldn't that be our focus as salespeople when we know the greatest opportunity for incremental business comes from our existing customer base? It's been proven time and again. Let's start believing it and acting accordingly.

346

We've already established that selling is a *battle* with our competitors. So then, let's introduce a key military practice to help us succeed. The *Debrief*. Harvard Business Review defines it best, *"...a structured learning process designed to continuously evolve plans while they're being executed...a way to learn quickly in rapidly changing situations and to address mistakes or changes on the [battle] field."* Could there be a more appropriate practice to apply to your sales efforts? Sales Managers & Sales Reps: Schedule your customer presentations mid to late morning, to be immediately followed by the *Debrief Lunch*.

347

In a field of numerous competitors, you occasionally need that outside-of-your-comfort-zone, flying-by-the-seat-of-your-pants, hair-on-fire, borderline out-of-control, tactical move which ensures you stay at the head of the pack. What moves of this type have you executed? Struggling to come up with examples? If so, you likely need to start pushing the envelope of what's possible in your selling efforts.

348

Focusing on service, cultivating loyalty, growing through referral, creating attraction with high value, leading in innovation, being easily discoverable, acting with fairness and dependability, and executing consistently are not new and novel business concepts. They are all elements of what has been classically known as a "Pull" strategy, which has been used for years by many successful companies as the core of their approach to the market. Companies like Caterpillar, Nike, and Apple. I'm sure you've heard of them…and you should strive to emulate many of their practices.

349

Trying to convince a customer that choosing your offering is the best decision, and by choosing the alternative they would be making a huge mistake, takes a lot of energy. Much more energy than allowing them to come to the point where they convince themselves of the fact. However, the latter requires more creativity, intelligence, patience, and risk-taking…but it's worth it! Craft your messaging, your value proposition, and your customer interactions in such a way that the client reaches the decision to buy from you through his own volition.

350

I've earlier mentioned my thoughts on the intellectual rigor required to maintain sustainable success in sales. This mental labor has a propensity to deplete you both physically and emotionally. It's important for the health of your career, and for you personally, that you be intentional about taking time to recharge. One of the more successful salespeople I was blessed to manage for several years early in my career, Dave, would occasionally walk into my office unannounced and bluntly inform me he would be taking a *mental health day* soon. I never begrudged it nor denied the request. I'm convinced it was, in part, what allowed him to stay at the top of his game. He never abused the privilege and seemed to always know exactly when it was needed. Self-awareness is the first and primary attribute of emotional intelligence.

351

If you spend significant commute time in your automobile, or an otherwise protracted amount of windshield time traveling to and from client appointments, don't waste those precious minutes or hours listening to talk radio. Instead, utilize the Bluetooth connectivity of your smartphone and leverage your solitude listening to a sales podcast, an audiobook, an inspirational keynote or Ted Talk, or whatever fires you up, allows you to learn, and helps you improve your craft.

352

The principles of Servant Leadership are not just reserved for the CEO or members of the executive team. Adopt a sales approach which includes listening, empathy, awareness, persuasion, conceptualization, foresight, and a commitment to the growth of your customer's business, and watch your success grow into uncharted territory.

353

As rewarding and lucrative as your sales career may be, don't let it be an end in itself. It should never be anything more than a means to an end, with the "*end*" being time spent with family and friends, personal enjoyment of sports or hobbies, investing for the future, helping and serving others, and other activities which will add meaning and purpose to your sales efforts, and contribute to the legacy you leave.

354

Sales Leaders: We talk frequently in business about sales enablement. It is certainly important to ensure your sales team is equipped with the tools and training necessary to win. However, in my experience, there is no greater method of empowerment for your people than genuine appreciation and honest encouragement. Give them both...Often!

355

There may be times when you want to force a *"Yes"* or *"No"* answer from your customer, but generally speaking, well-thought, open-ended questions will give you more of the information you are looking for and will give the customer an opportunity to reveal where they need the most help. It will also allow them to answer in terms of your offered solution. There's a methodology to proper questioning and it's deserving of your time and focus. Email me for a free tutorial.

356

It is common to be overwhelmed when just starting out in your sales career. You will find yourself faced with learning product, application, pricing, industry practices, and customer information…and not just learning those things, but understanding how they all work together. There are competing philosophies regarding how to start. One of the more popular is to learn as much as you possibly can before making that first customer visit. My personal experience has been that I've learned more quickly, the earlier I could get in front of customers. Being faced with questions I did not know the answers to, accelerated my comprehension and greatly increased my retention. Perhaps it might work the same for you. Step out and give it a go!

357

When you enjoy what you do, your learning curve flattens out and you advance more quickly. Pick a product or an industry you have a genuine interest in or affinity for and you will likely experience rapid progression in both your achievement and acumen.

358

I don't care how busy you are…and neither does your customer. No one is so busy they cannot return a call within 24 hours. That's an inconvenient truth that flows from the C-Suite to front office reception. Don't use a call screener, don't postpone difficult conversations, and never refuse to call someone back. Keep yourself on the frontline as much as you can. It helps aid in the pursuit of knowing your customer better than anyone else.

359

Companies get sold, careers change, products improve or become obsolete, and certain other things in life just happen. Don't fear or be anxious about any of it. The way you treat people is universal and will be a core driver of your success no matter where life takes you.

360

It's dangerous to assume the product the customer is currently using is exactly what she needs. There's also danger in asking the wrong questions. Too often, the weak salesperson queries the customer on the specifications of her current solution and simply offers his brand and latest version of it. What if the customer's application has changed? What if she wants to future-proof the next acquisition by purchasing something capable of expansion? What if the previous salesperson didn't perform his due diligence and sold a less optimal solution? ALWAYS question, examine, and observe to uncover need. Then, work backwards to arrive at the best solution to meet that need…ALWAYS.

361

Draft a *Performance Guarantee* document that outlines the support promises from every customer-facing department. Include a "Direct Access" section with the caveat that any concerns which remain unresolved after 24 hours will be on the appropriate executive leader's desk for immediate attention. Have that individual affix their signature at the bottom. Don't just talk about how great you are at taking care of customers...put it in writing.

362

Enablement, Agility, Leaning in, Big Data, Thought Leadership, CX…these are some of the business buzzwords of the day. Perhaps never before has there been so much repackaging and renaming of time-honored business principles. Don't be anxious if you happen not to speak in the current business vernacular. All the foregoing means is…be adequately prepared, position yourself to quickly pivot in response to circumstances, invest yourself into your opportunities, harness the power of technology, dedicate yourself to creativity, and understand that how you take care of your customers will have the greatest influence on whether or not they purchase from you again.

363

I was 10 years into my career when I attended a sales seminar and was challenged with a question regarding the last time I had read a book on selling. It was convicting… and it was also the beginning of what has become a dedication to continually learning and perfecting my craft. After all, it's what I've chosen for my livelihood, it's how I provide for my family, it's what allows me to build long-term business relationships and friendships, and it's a medium by which I can serve others. I recommend allowing it to become the same for you, and hope this book helps you take the next step in that journey.

364

If there was a way to accurately predict the future, your success in sales would of course, be unlimited. As a bonus, I can make TWO predictions for you right now. First, your sales career will one day come to an end. And second, so will your life. Live well… by being a person of integrity and character. Leave well…having wisely spent time on the things that matter. It won't be your trophies, plaques, and sales awards you will want to be surrounded by at the end. It will be family & friends and those you love.

365

"Do you not know that in a race all the runners run, but only one gets the prize? Run in such a way as to get the prize"

– The Apostle Paul